Share this book ...

"I am sharing this book

My Name	Date

SolePath

the path to purpose and a beautiful life

Dr. Debra Ford Msc.D

Copyright © 2013 Dr. Debra Ford Msc.D

Author:
Dr. Debra Ford Msc.D, inspirational teacher and spiritual mystic
Editor:
John C. Ford M, charismatic adventurer and intellectual lateral thinker
Cover design:
Celeste Needham, intuitive builder and intuitive creator
Author photo:
Vanessa Sikomas, spiritual balance and spiritual mystic
Publisher: Energy Mountain Inc.
716 brookpark drive sw, calgary, ab, Canada, t2w 2x4
T: 403.998.0191
E: info@SolePath.org
W: www.SolePath.org

Library and Archives Canada Cataloguing in Publication

Ford, Debra, 1957-, author
    SolePath : the path to purpose and a beautiful life
/ Dr. Debra Ford.

Issued in print and electronic formats.
ISBN 978-0-9784271-7-7 (pbk.).—ISBN 978-0-9784271-8-4 (pdf)

    . Self-realization. 2. Success--Psychological aspects.
    I.   Title.

BF637.S4F66 2013   158.1   C2013-904854-5
                              C2013-904855-3

DEDICATION

For John, Joel, Adam and Elizabeth

"THIS BOOK IS THE STORY OF SOLEPATH AND OF DEBRA'S
ABILITY TO HEAR THE TEACHINGS OF SOLEPATH. SHE
MODELS FOR OTHERS HOW THIS CAN BE DONE. SO THAT
THOSE WHO READ THIS BOOK ARE INSPIRED TOWARDS THEIR
OWN BODY OF WORK; THE GREAT TRUTH THAT WILL BE
THEIRS."

SETH

SolePath
the path to purpose and a beautiful life

Written on the 27th floor of the Island Pacific Hotel in Hong Kong, between Saturday May 26 and Saturday June 1, 2013. Dr. Debra and John spent an inspiring week in Hong Kong at this hotel, room 2613.

Hong Kong – one of the throat chakras of the world; a great place for communication.

CONTENTS

ACKNOWLEDGMENTS

This work would not ever have been manifest without the love, support and countless hours that John has dedicated to our work together. My deep gratitude for your role in this teaching; you hold my heart.

To my sons, Joel and Adam, my deep thankfulness for your support and for always trusting me and loving me just as I am, your very different mother.

Seth calls her his butterfly; and I call her my wingman; she has no equal. Without her unquestioning support and true friendship I would so often have been lost. My friend, Deneen, you are a gift to me and to SolePath. Thank you for sharing your intuitive creator beauty and spiritual balance flow with me.

For Terry, an intellectual lateral thinker and inspirational manager, who is almost completely unaware of the strength and support that he provides to both John and I and the SolePath work. Our conservative, meat and potatoes guy, who is one of our greatest enthusiasts, deep gratitude.

For Celeste, an intuitive builder and intuitive creator who has added so much beauty to SolePath with her designs, including this beautiful book cover and timeline diagram, my deepest thanks for your patient nurturing of our friendship. Building on her life experience and manifesting ideas as she helps others create their own beautiful lives.

To Eric, an intuitive creator and inspirational humanitarian, who with his SolePath and these amazing gifts and greatness has created our SolePath website, thank you.

For Jill, an intuitive creator and spiritual warrior, who walked my early path with me through the teachings and understandings of space energy. Together with Jill I learned how to apply this sacred teaching onto the energy of our life.

For Leigh Ann, an intuitive builder and inspirational manager, who was involved in SolePath in the early stages and helped with the understanding of how SolePath manifests in peoples lives. Leigh Ann made a big commitment to SolePath, and Seth has been a great supporter of Leigh Ann's efforts.

I would also like to acknowledge these incredible souls who have become part of our SolePath work, who are in the process of creating their own great truth as they live in their LightPaths and connect to the wisdom of their soul.

For Tanis, a spiritual balance and spiritual mystic who from her LightPaths is connecting and expanding her yoga nidra work to provide direction as each of us undertakes the very difficult work of reprogramming the beliefs and habits that hold us back from our life of joy.

For Vanessa, a double spiritual, a balance and a mystic, who is discovering her ability to clearly communicate difficult spiritual understandings. Knowing that this will be her perfect manifestation, helping others to understand invisible concepts and encouraging them towards metaphysical study. Seth has also thanked Vanessa for making this SolePath book a part of her spiritual book club, for assisting him in his work.

For Shyla, a spiritual mystic and spiritual warrior who is connecting to her great truth; as she learns to trust and understand her ability to uncover information on individual ill health and assist with solutions and therapy for healing.

For Susan, an intuitive hunter and charismatic influencer, and her partner Rick, an intuitive builder and inspirational conformist, who are called to seek truth, help others create plans for a fulfilling life, and inspire them to choose to build thriving lives after major life changes, including addiction recovery.

For Kathy, a compassionate facilitator and spiritual mystic, who understands community and is assisting others who are working with the law of attraction, helping them find direction for their intentions.

For Stephanie, a compassionate healer and inspirational humanitarian who is allowing her 'cause' and gifts of healing others to unfold.

For Kael, an inspirational teacher and spiritual balance, who is guiding others to peace and to purpose through her mentoring, teaching and counseling.

For Louise, a compassionate healer and spiritual warrior who is choosing what she would like to heal, and flexing her psychic muscles.

For Dr. Krista, a spiritual mystic and compassionate healer, who is born to combine her spiritual wisdom with her naturopathic doctor healing skills and assisting others to physical, emotional and mental health.

For Ronna, a charismatic leader and inspirational teacher who with her sparkle and charisma and extraordinary ability to communicate, is breaking new ground in her community leading the initiative to combine holistic learning within the traditional school system.

For Michael, an intuitive hunter and spiritual warrior, one of the SolePath early adopters, who is proof that when you are ready the SolePath truth unfolds.

For Judy, another double intuitive, hunter and creator, who understands our need for ritual and ceremony in life. Who is sharing with community through her rhythm drumming practice and providing a beautiful environment of peace and safety for others.

For Ed, a compassionate healer and intuitive builder, a born healer who is focusing on healing disease rather than treating the symptoms. Serving his own patients and also providing possibilities for other practitioners to heal the sick and injured.

For Lucy, an intuitive hunter and inspirational manager, who knows that her passion and her work is deeply connected to the earth and the environment.

For Shamir, a compassionate facilitator and compassionate healer, who is creating spiritual healing within the extraordinary community that he is building.

For Janet, a charismatic adventurer and charismatic gladiator, who simply knows that it is possible to live a better life, to be a happier person, to strive for more, and is sharing her truth with others.

For Dr. Karen, an intuitive creator and inspirational conformist who is building on her traditional chinese medicine practice and the research of her father to create new healing modalities.

For Wanda, an intellectual lateral thinker and spiritual warrior, who along with her friend Shirley, an inspirational teacher and spiritual balance, have started a SolePath community in their neighbourhood. Providing a spiritual sanctuary for like-minded people.

And for you ...

INTRODUCTION

"THIS BOOK IS THE STORY OF SOLEPATH AND OF DEBRA'S
ABILITY TO HEAR THE TEACHINGS OF SOLEPATH. SHE
MODELS FOR OTHERS HOW THIS CAN BE DONE. SO THAT
THOSE WHO READ THIS BOOK ARE INSPIRED TOWARDS THEIR
OWN BODY OF WORK; THE GREAT TRUTH THAT WILL BE
THEIRS."
SETH

June 2006. I was standing directly in front of a closed door
with the dark passageway spreading out to my left and my
right. I was standing still and looking up at the very wide and
very tall door. Out of the corner of my eye, to my left, I saw a
young man in a white tunic and pale blue skirt leaning with
his back up against the wall of the corridor. He stood on one
leg with his other knee bent and the sole of his right foot up
against the wall. He had curly blonde hair, was slim, early
thirties, and seemed relaxed resting up against the wall. He
turned his head to me and said "What kept you so long? We
have been waiting." He signaled for me to open the door. I
did not.

September 2006. Once again, I was in the dark passageway
outside the door. He was there and as if it was the most
natural thing in the world, opened the door for me and we
walked through together. His chatty cheerfulness seemed to
be a deliberate distraction although all I could hear was
sound coming out of his mouth, no distinct words.

He stood really close by as if to reassure me and then clearly
said "here we go!" I squinted up my eyes and replied "I can't
see anything, it is too bright." With calm encouragement and
making sure I could feel him standing next to me, he
whispered "wait just a minute".

My eyes got used to the brightness and slowly focused. We were in a long white corridor with tall white doors down either side; very tall doors with round doorknobs; about six or eight doors on either side of the corridor, all them closed. The doors on the left attracted me more.

The corridor was filled with bright white light. Brightness everywhere, not coming from light fixtures but seeming to be all around and everywhere, no shadows. White walls, white doors, white door knobs, white flooring and all of this leading up a slight incline to a commanding white building at the top of the rise. Huge sweeping steps, also white, led up to the building which had columns on either side of the entrance. It was roman or greek looking, imposing, majestic, beautiful.

As we stood at the beginning of the white corridor, he said "this is where we are now; at the beginning; be positive; enjoy this unfolding; I am with you for the whole journey."

And so began my journey with Peter my first non-physical guide, the weird mystical journey of my life that has resulted in the manifesting of the original body of work called SolePath.

The purpose of this SolePath book is to inspire you towards your great truth. Because I know that you have a teaching within you, I know that you have a body of work to manifest, I know that your great truth is waiting, I know that you are ready to serve.

Ready?

Dr. Debra

SECTION 1 - BEGINNINGS

- A mysterious life
- Beliefs and philosophy
- Dr. Debra's guides
- Origins of SolePath
- What is SolePath

Dying, its like being in a fog with the lights turned on. You can't see a thing but it is very bright. Even the sound is both expanded and muffled. I know, I have been there. This knowing became a big part of the creation of the SolePath original body of work.
Dr. Debra

Dr. Debra Ford Msc.D

SECTION 1 - BEGINNINGS

A mysterious life

There has always been a deep yearning inside of me to understand the mysteries of life. As a child I would daydream about what it would be like to be inside the body of someone else; what it might feel like to be male; a person of a different race; live in a handicapped body. When walking to school, I would imagine a parallel me, walking to school in a different place or a different time. I thought this was what everyone did.

I spent years chasing light worms down the sidewalk, trying to catch the sparkles that were in the air, wondering why others couldn't see the multi-coloured air around them. Adults would often say to me, what are you looking at, what do you see, don't look at me that way!

As a little girl I kept a dark secret about abuse in my family. I was a fixer and my father threatened me with the break up of our family and also hurting my little sister, unless I kept 'our little secret'. I was prepared to sacrifice my emotional and physical health for what I thought was best for those I loved.

My SolePath braid is inspirational teacher and spiritual mystic, entwined with dark compassionate healer. My spiritual mystic is that part of me that had the instinctive understanding that we choose who we are born to be, that we are more than our physical body, and that who we really are isn't what we appear to be. My inspirational teacher is that child who could clearly see others. My dark compassionate healer is the little girl who thought that to save her family, she had to sacrifice herself.

My SolePath helps me understand the mysteries of my life; those experiences that give me joy, those that create my emotional, mental and physical pain, those that provide me with choice for my personal growth, for my perfect eternal soul's evolution. But mostly my SolePath is the way that I navigate my life towards love, happiness and my life's purpose; the way that I live a meaningful life. It is my internal sub-conscious navigation.

I am not a charismatic adventurer and intellectual lateral thinker, like my husband John; he is all about the new and innovation. Nor a compassionate facilitator and intuitive builder like my eldest son Joel; he is a community builder who creates possibilities. Nor an intuitive hunter and charismatic leader like my youngest son Adam; his gift is truth seeking and lighting up our world with his sparkle and charisma.

I have my own unique gifts and greatness. The original body of work called SolePath is my life's work. As a spiritual mystic I connect and as an inspirational teacher I know how to communicate. This is who I was born to be and SolePath is a direct manifestation of my gifts and greatness.

What Seth calls your great truth is also accessible and lives within your unique gifts and greatness. Each of us has a SolePath and we are all so different and so important to our world.   Knowing my SolePath makes sense of my life's unique experiences; it creates those 'wow! that explains everything' moments; that deep understanding of the meaning of my life and enabled the manifestation of SolePath, my life's work.

My SolePath is the guidance for my life; it provides the navigation system for living a beautiful life; it allows me to be who I was born to be. And I want to own and be recognized for my gifts and greatness, my unique weirdness, my ability to make a difference in the world.

And I need you to own yours, to be absolutely, completely and uniquely you. To be recognized as being wonderful in

Dr. Debra Ford Msc.D

your own way as you live your meaningful life that is entirely different from mine. Because when you step into your greatness who knows what that could mean for our world?

Beliefs and philosophy

Here's what I believe; this does not have to match what you believe, but it will help put the sacred SolePath body of work into context.

Firstly, we are perfect eternal souls having a physical experience and this is not the first time that we have come to our beautiful planet. We choose to come to earth to evolve through experiencing contrast; what we don't want.

We come to experience the struggles, the negativity, the mental, emotional and physical pain, so that we can experience deliberately choosing what we do want in our lives; joy, love, positive choices and behaviours. To experience highs and lows, yin and yang, ups and downs, joy and pain, because choosing joy in the face of the difficulties of our life is how we grow.

Secondly, there is a detailed planning process that occurs before each incarnation. We choose all of the elements of our life to create the perfect opportunity for our soul's evolution. Everything about our lives is carefully chosen to provide us with the perfect life experience. Before we are born we create a plan for our lives and this plan includes our SolePath and our life circumstances and brings influences from our ancestry and past lives. We come to earth to grow, to evolve as a perfect eternal soul and we create the perfect plan, including the perfect SolePath that will allow us to do this.

Thirdly, our life is planned in collaboration with those who love us; our soul community. There isn't anything in our plan, in our life, that we can't cope with. We are loved, deeply cared for and watched over by our soul community and all of what we are experiencing benefits our whole community. We are safe and all is well.

Exit points

Our life plan contains exit points, those moments when we can choose to go home, back to our soul community. The number of exit points we write into our plan is a purely individual choice and I am sure as you think back over your life you can recall those close shaves, those times when you know you could have died. Exit points may manifest as near misses in accidents, serious health issues where you healed yourself and in a myriad other ways. They are lifelines for when we can go back home to our soul community where we are loved, nurtured and completely safe.

When in vitro, during pregnancy, we usually create frequent exit points as we are sampling, testing and settling into being an expanded energy in a confined physical body. This explains why there are so many miscarriages. Souls are coming into a body, figuratively taking it for a test drive and going home if they desire. John and I had two miscarriages and I know the depth of grief felt when the baby you have yearned for dies, but it makes it easier for me to understand that I was providing another perfect eternal soul the opportunity to have their experience. I know that when I created my plan this was an experience that we agreed to, my babies and I.

One of our miscarriages was late in the pregnancy and in 1984 our daughter Elizabeth decided not to be born. I have subsequently learned that her work, as a non-physical guide, is shepherding souls as they take up residence in a body. Loving them, counseling them as they get used to these confines and bringing them back home to their non-physical community if they need to.

Elizabeth needed to experience a pregnancy herself to help her with her soul purpose of assisting souls coming into physical form, and John and I, as her parents, agreed to participate in that experience with her. Elizabeth has taught us that it is much more difficult for a soul to move into the confines of a physical body than to leave at the point of death and go back home to those who love us.

One of the exit points I wrote into my life's plan became a near death experience. I was 14 years old and very excited getting ready for the school dance. My parents had agreed that I could go and rides to and from the dance had been organized. My dad would drive my three friends and I to the dance and the mother of one of my friends would be there at the appointed time to drive us home. We lived in kimberley, south africa, a quiet, dusty diamond-mining town. My father was a prominent minister of one of the churches in town and apart from my church activities; the school dance was a big event in my life.

I don't really remember much about the dance, I am sure we all had fun together. But I do remember the ride home. My friend's mother had a very old, heavy 4x4 — one of those really designed for life in the bush, not the softer versions that people drive in cities now. It was black and very dirty — their family spent a lot of time in the wilder areas that encroached right up to the outskirts of our town. We bundled into the 4x4, her son in the front and the rest of us in the back and drove through the deserted late night streets, dropping friends at home, until there were just 3 of us left in the car. I was sitting in the back behind the driver, which was on the right side of the vehicle — in south africa we drove on the left side of the road. The muddy 4x4 crawled along in the dark. slowly but surely. I felt it sway with that long pause between gears, each time she changed the old fashioned manual gearshift. I started to drop off to sleep - it had been an exciting night.

My next recollection was the incredible force of the impact of another vehicle smashing into the 4x4. I don't remember feeling anything, it was more the sound and a very particular smell; a smell that I distinctly remember and have never smelt again. The speeding vehicle crashed into us on the same side that the driver and I were sitting.

It was at this moment that I realized that I was watching what was happening rather than being a part of it. I first saw my body flying around in the back of the 4x4; this old bush vehicle didn't have any seatbelts in the back seat. I noticed my black coat, even the seam running down the back of the coat. I noticed my jeans; I had taken such care getting dressed for the dance. My patient mother hadn't commented on the clothes left strewn around my bedroom, as I had tried on one outfit after another. I noticed my long hair flying around my head and even thought — oh it really looks good, I don't see it from the back that often!

As I watched myself I realized that the 4x4 had spun into an electrical pole and knocked it down; the broken electrical wires were sparking around the vehicle and on the road. The other vehicle was so smashed up that it was unrecognizable, and the four teenagers in that small car did not seem to be moving. My friend's mother was slumped over her steering wheel, her head was turned towards the window with her eyes open, but she was very still. I did not notice what had happened to my friend.

The smell and sounds were real and very present. It was like being a bird and looking down at events that didn't really have that much to do with me. I really was the peaceful observer of the whole wreckage scene.

My focus moved back to me and away from the scene below, away from my body, and I was enveloped in white light. My

Dr. Debra Ford Msc.D

best description is that it was like looking ahead into a fog with your vehicle lights on. It was a dense white mist and I was moving through it. Everything became very quiet and muted and I felt like I was speeding ahead, but not moving my body. Similar to being on an escalator in a tunnel; I knew that I was moving, but wasn't actually doing anything myself, just resting in the white light and knowing that I was going somewhere fast! At this stage I had no further awareness of my body or of the chaos of the car accident. I just felt good, I knew where I was going and what I was doing.

Next thing, I said out loud "I am not finished yet." I didn't see who I was speaking with but I did have a feeling of incredible love and peacefulness. I didn't notice that I was answering a question, no one seemed to have asked me a question, I simply said out loud "I am not finished yet".

My next recollection was waking up down the road from the accident, sitting on the curb and using my coat to brush away the blood that was running down my face and neck. I also have a vague memory of running down the middle of the road, but this isn't as clear for me. A kind man and his wife, woken by the impact of the crash, shepherded me into their home for a cup of tea and called my parents.

All of the teenagers in the other vehicle died in the crash that night. My parents attended their funerals in the week that followed. The driver of the 4x4, my friend's mother, spent almost three months in hospital recovering from her severe injuries. My friend walked away without a scratch and I suffered only soft tissue bruising, a laceration to my head and my back and spent just one week recovering physically.

As I grew into adulthood, I was careful to whom I mentioned this childhood near death experience. My fundamental christian upbringing didn't give me any clues as to what the meaning of it could be. As I processed my childhood abuse and the contradiction of my father's life as a man of god, I decided in my late teens to leave the church and to separate myself from this rigid upbringing. It is only since my spiritual searching revived in 1995, that this near death experience has made sense to me, that it has become part of my deep understanding that we make a plan for our life before we are born.

I did believe that life continues after we leave earth, my sunday school classes made certain that I knew all about heaven and hell. But what I have deeply come to know is that not only did I exist before I came to earth as a perfect eternal soul, but that I created a detailed plan for this life experience on earth that included my SolePath. All of us write exit points into our plans and one of mine transpired on the night of that fatal accident and I didn't choose to end my earthly life experience at that time, I was not finished.

Dr. Debra's Guides

SolePath is the work of my council of seven. I was first introduced to them during surgery in August 2006. While under anesthetic I saw a group of beings standing behind the surgeon; one was larger than the others who were grouped around him. I had only just met Peter (who I introduced you to in the introduction to this book) in the June of that year, but he seemed part of the group and comfortable around them, so I decided that I would feel safe too.

They looked a little like the expected version of an alien with the large sloping eyes, oval faces and white or light grey wispy bodies. I felt very loved and watched over by them and remembered them vividly when the surgery anesthetic wore off.

I saw them as light energies, not too scary or real looking, just intangible enough to make them seem other wordly.

Dr. Debra Ford Msc.D

Back then, I didn't know if they had a purpose in my life, but I loved seeing them even without understanding who they were or what they were doing.

Three years later, in 2009 the SolePath body of work was downloaded. I learned later that it is a teaching from them, my council of seven.

In June 2011 a different guide arrived. She told me that her name is Jane and unlike the council of seven she appears in a physical body as a woman, except that unlike Peter, she is bigger than a normal size person. She is older than I am and is always sitting in an armchair; has a wise matriarchal energy and mostly peers at me over the top of her reading glasses.

At first I was thoroughly intimidated by her, she seemed so stern, so big, so real, so human. I was more used to my non-physical companions having a wispier look, like my council; or being kinder, gentler and more compassionate, like Peter. She was just there, in her chair, in my bedroom not saying anything.

One day, out of the blue, Jane told me that we would be working together on SolePath and right from that beginning my interactions with her were very different. With my council of seven the communication is so subtle, I feel that I am interpreting what I imagine they are saying, I spend many contented hours mulling over what it is we are conversing on, and I love the ambiguity.

With Jane it is the same as having a conversation with a live person. I say something and she answers me right back, I don't have to interpret and boy can she be direct. It began with thoughts in my head, I thought the question and received the thought answer right back.

In September 2011 Jane introduced me to Seth. He too presented himself as a very human looking male. He is also big and just stood there, behind Jane's chair, quietly for four months. They were very relaxed together and I just got used to his presence, to him always being there. He never said anything and I never asked what he was doing there; it just felt okay.

Two weeks after another surgery in January 2012, coincidentally from the same surgeon, Seth and Jane started speaking with me. Beginning February 10, 2012, night after night I would wake up around 3am and feel compelled to sit with my notepad and pen asking questions and writing down answers from Seth and Jane. My husband John would know that I had been up for hours each night as he would find the notebook open to the page on the dining room table when he woke in the morning.

Seth and Jane started providing guidance on expanding the SolePath body of work, they answered questions about business strategy and provided personal relationship and health guidance. It became an easy and familiar pattern, I wrote down my question and clearly heard their answer. In my head, I could hear the difference in their voices and knew when it was Seth answering or when Jane was speaking.

This writing was a process that I was very comfortable with. I was not comfortable with becoming what others label as a channeler; it felt scary, egotistical, decidedly weird and I just felt unsafe. I was also slowly learning who Seth and Jane were, from the 1970's, and that also made me nervous.

I had heard of Seth and Jane once before, a brief mention at an Abraham-Hicks conference John and I had attended, and had not read more than a snippet of their earlier work. My repeated lament was, why couldn't you be some other guides, guides who are equally wise, but not so well known.

A friend showed me the beautiful portrait of Seth painted in the 70's and I didn't recognize him at all, it is not how I see

Dr. Debra Ford Msc.D

him. Jane doesn't look like her photographs either; she looks like judy dench to me. In the beginning that is how I would describe her; 'judy dench is peering at me over her glasses again'. Seth has darker hair, he is swarthy, slim and early fifties I would say. Handsome in an experienced older guy kind of way. I think he loves the look, very attractive, but am not sure he likes his dress style, he wears roman looking robes, comfortable but not very sexy.

Little did I know that this writing was just a short step away from becoming the voice for Seth, from speaking his words as he urges us to service using our SolePaths gifts.

My dear friend Deneen arrived at our home one day and said, 'I want to speak with Seth'. No problem, I would do what I always did, write down her questions and that night at the predictable 3am, receive the answers for her. That was not what she meant. She sat me down, turned on the computer audio recording and I said, "it's Thursday May 24, 2012 and this is a live download, the first live download from Seth" and so it began.

I am not consciously present when I speak for Seth. Rather I am certainly present and sitting there with my eyes closed, but I don't usually remember more than a few ideas of what he has said. If the download is for SolePath or for my family, I listen to the recording afterwards to hear the guidance.

When Seth speaks, he often says, she can't find my word and indeed most of the time he gives me the general concept using lots of visual images and I try to put what he is wanting to communicate into coherent english. He does correct me if I don't get it right and sometimes we go around and around until he is satisfied.

I distinctly remember him showing me a leaf one day and wanting me to tell the mother of a young son that he needed a higher dosage of echinacea. It certainly took time for me to connect to that one.

One client who came to speak with Seth asked him if he would like a cigar and a stiff drink during her session. Seth said that Jane had obliged him when he spoke through her, but that I was not likely to. I must be a lot more uptight than Jane and we have taken time, Seth and I, finding our way to a comfortable relationship.

Seth is completely single minded. Underneath all that he speaks of, he is urging us to service. Sometimes he is kind, sometimes he uses tough love, and sometimes he says things that I would never say. I have been told expressly by him that I cannot censor his words and when I listen back to the recordings I can say that on a few occasions I have been mortified by his direct approach.

Jane is different, I have not as yet become her 'voice' and I don't know if I ever will; she has not said that she wants this. To give you an idea of what it is like to interact with her, here is a typical conversation between us. This is the last conversation I had with her while in Hong Kong, May 25, 2013, just before this book was written. If you wish, for me you can take on a whiny tone and for Jane a no-nonsense rather irritated manner:

> *Debra: I am lost? Really?*
>
> *Jane: Okay let's say you need a refocus. It's time for creation.*
>
> *Debra: How did you do it? Make time for the writing?*
>
> *Jane: Scheduling. Deliberate conscious effort.*
>
> *Debra: I heard that you disbelieved your Seth connection and downloads at the end.*

Dr. Debra Ford Msc.D

Jane: Doubted. Wouldn't you? It was so new then. Good thing it was just after the sixties when all things weird and different were happening.

Debra: You said, or Seth said, that no one would ever channel him again.

Jane: So? He's changed his mind. There's nothing to be afraid of. He is supporting the work, our work, the council's work. Want him to go away?

Debra: No!!! What's next?

Jane: Just write the damn book! The SolePath book.

Sisterly advice, familiar inspiring, nothing soft about her. She is a straight talker and I love Jane.

One thing, I am really good at doing is trusting the guidance, doing what is asked of me, and this book was written as fast and as easily as the sacred SolePaths were downloaded back in 2009. One week for the writing, another few for the editing and here it is. Trust.

Seth and Jane play an integral part in guiding the SolePath work and I have subsequently learned that both Jane and I are part of the council of seven. I have also learned that Seth is engaged with others, assisting them with their metaphysical work on our planet. His primary focus is guiding us to service.

2012 and 2013 have been a time of major energetic shift on our planet and we have also, since the taurus solar eclipse in may 2013, completed a major 19-year cycle. Not only are we individually examining old values that no longer serve us but we are also changing the paradigm of our world; the energy on the planet is supporting your great truth, the world is ready.

Here is what Seth says about the changing energy on our planet.

THIS IS INDEED A TIME OF TRANSITION. A TIME OF MOVING FROM ONE PLACE OF EXPERIENCE TO A DIFFERENT ONE. AND YOU ARE DOING THIS TOGETHER AS A COLLECTIVE. THERE IS A VIBRATION CHANGE WITHIN YOU THAT IS ALTERING THE VIBRATION OF ALL OF YOU. YOU ARE ALL ON EARTH FOR INDIVIDUAL EXPERIENCE AND FOR COLLECTIVE EXPERIENCE. AND THE COLLECTIVE EXPERIENCE SHIFTS DEPENDING ON WHAT HAS GONE BEFORE. NOW, LIGHT IS NEEDED ON YOUR PLANET, ALL SOULS KNOW THIS.

THIS HAS JUST BEGUN. A NEW ENERGY IS UNFOLDING. YOU, SOULS ON EARTH AT THIS TIME, ARE THE PIONEERS. ALL IS WELL. MORE AND MORE WILL BEGIN TO ASK, "HOW MAY I SERVE?" THE ENERGY WILL MOVE FROM 'ME' TO 'US'. IT IS THE DESTINY OF YOUR PLANET.

OUR WORK IS STILL AT THE BEGINNING. WE ARE THANKFUL THAT THE ENERGETIC SHIFT ON THE PLANET IS SUPPORTING THE CHANGE THAT MUST COME ABOUT. YOU, ALL OF YOU, ARE OUR LIGHT WORKERS. BUT IT IS A LOVING WORK, A WORK FILLED WITH JOY, A WORK THAT IS FUN. WE SENSE A GREAT DEAL OF SERIOUSNESS, OF BURDEN, OF WEIGHT THAT IS NOT NEEDED.

THERE IS A SENSE OF LONGING, A YEARNING FOR PURPOSE THAT YOU ARE WITNESSING THROUGH THE SOLEPATH WORK. THIS WILL GROW AND GROW WITH MORE AND MORE PEOPLE LOOKING FOR THE REASON FOR EXISTENCE ON YOUR PLANET. OUR HELP IS ESSENTIAL NOW. WE ARE FULLY ENGAGED. TOGETHER WITH ALL OF YOU. IT IS TIME.

THERE IS SOME THOUGHT THAT GOOD DEEDS ARE BIG DEEDS AND THAT IS TOO MUCH FOR AN INDIVIDUAL TO UNDERTAKE. BUT ANY POSITIVE ENERGY, DIRECTED IN ANY WAY IS FUNDAMENTALLY IMPORTANT TO THE PLANET. ENERGETIC WORK AT ALL LEVELS IS VITAL AND IT HAS THE SAME VALUE, THE SAME WORTH, THE SAME IMPORTANCE. A SIMPLE DESIRE, FOLLOWED BY A POSITIVE ACTION, TO MAKE SOMEONE ELSE FEEL BETTER, IS WHAT YOU ARE CALLED TO DO. KIND WORDS, TO FRIENDS AND TO STRANGERS, DELIBERATE

ACTIONS WITH INTENT, FOR POSITIVE CHANGE.

IT IS INDEED A TIME OF CHANGE. THERE IS PERFECTION HERE, AS
LIFE ON YOUR PLANET COULD NOT CONTINUE AS IT WAS GOING.
CHANGE IS UNDERWAY. TRULY, ALL IS WELL.

SETH

Joseph Campbell wrote way back in the 1970's, that what has
gone wrong with our society is that the focus has moved away
from the act to the execution of the act; from the activity —
what we are doing, to the doing of the activity — how we are
doing it; from the what to the how.

In this way we have no longer found it necessary to question
what we are doing, but simply to focus on how it is being
done. We live without fundamental compassion and
common sense and acts of atrocity against people, animals
and our beautiful planet have found willing participants and
followers. How often have we heard 'its not personal, its
only business'?

It is a time of energetic change on our planet, a time when
the energy supports each of us caring about all of us. It will
become personal; it will not be okay to do someone or
something down in the name of what is best for profit and
for business.

Of course it will take time, but we are heading for a new
normal where it will become less and less common that we pit
ourselves against each other; where we will collaborate for
the good of community. We will ask 'how may I serve', and
this is the focus of Seth's work.

Origins of SolePath

My deep longing to understand the mysteries of life continued into adulthood. I have asked where we have come from and where we are going. I have wondered how and when it all began and how and when it will end. I know deep inside myself, that unless we are more than we appear to be; unless we are more than our physical body, then this existence on earth simply doesn't make sense.

I am an ordained minister and doctor of metaphysical science. Metaphysics is the philosophical enquiry into the nature of existence and my joy comes from exploring what I call the five fundamental questions of life. Who am I? What am I doing here? Who will I be in relation to what is going on around me? Where do I come from? Where am I going?

My spiritual mystic had spent many years joyfully searching for the answers to these fundamental questions of life and in the process, to engage my inspirational teacher, I was awarded my doctorate in metaphysical counseling in September 2007. I loved my clients and put my heart and soul into teaching what I had learned during my metaphysical explorations.

During the first session intake for each new client I would ask why they had come to see me. Nine times out of ten the answer would be, "I am lost. I don't know who I am. I don't know what my life is all about". We would spend our sessions working on these fundamental questions of life, learning metaphysical tools and working on creating their life of joy.

After six months, it was my normal practice to complete an updated evaluation and when I asked what we needed to work on, the answer would often be the same 'I don't know who I am, I don't know what I am doing, my life has no meaning'.

I knew that there was something missing from the

Dr. Debra Ford Msc.D

counseling. Although I had a busy practice, my clients did not seem to be making any real progress in their lives. They would leave my office feeling ready to take on their life and then return for their next session on their hands and knees; never seeming to move forward towards creating a meaningful life filled with real joy, peace and contentment.

My dark compassionate healer became thoroughly engaged. I just couldn't seem to heal and fix my clients and along with deep frustration, I also became very despondent and fatigued.

As a means of escape and rejuvenation I attended a week long meditation intensive at the monroe institute in virginia, usa. An extraordinary experience called gateway voyage during which I spent hours and hours each day connecting with my guides and exploring the metaphysical.

The gateway voyage was a journey of spiritual exploring that gave structure to what was an unfocused and meandering process for me. I became familiar with how to connect directly with Peter and my council of seven in a mind awake and body asleep state. I visited the place where all non-physical guides are found, a state that monroe calls expanded awareness. I explored past and future lives as they showed me how to expand beyond time, in a place of no time and of all time.

Monroe gateway gave me focus and structure for my spiritual exploring and enhanced my ability to connect to the wisdom of non-physical. I found that images came more easily and I trusted and developed a better way to interpret what I was connecting to and seeing. I became and still am a hemi-sync junkie.

It was about two months after my visit to the monroe institute that John and I were hosting hemi-sync meditation evenings in our home. Before each session I would ask participants to write their intention for their evening meditation. On June 24, 2009, after a particularly frustrating day in my counseling room, I wrote in my meditation journal "WHO AM I ?!?", capital letters and many exclamation marks. I was completely defeated by my apparent inability to help my clients' answer that question and make any real and lasting progress towards creating their meaningful life.

I relaxed into my meditation and imagine my surprise when I received the answer. It certainly wouldn't be an overstatement to say that I was shocked by the clarity that this answer gave me. As a general rule, I love living my life in the grey areas, in the space where there are no concrete answers, in the pause between the in and out breath. Yet here was black and white clarity about who I was born to be and I loved it.

I also learned during this meditation that everyone could receive this same clarity; we could all know this answer. When we decide to come to earth and have a physical life incarnation, we have a plan, there is a path that our soul wants to walk, a path that will provide us with the life experience our perfect eternal soul intended, a path that guides us to purpose and a meaningful life. And we can know what this is.

From the next day, my birthday, June 25, 2009, I sat down at my computer and wrote blindly for two weeks. At the end of each day I would say to John, 'I don't know what I am writing' but with his encouragement I kept writing for hours each day and the 22 SolePaths were downloaded. I knew that this work wasn't mine as I was writing about things that I had not studied, read about or heard about before.

I do state that I am the creator of SolePath because I haven't found a better way to say it, but SolePath simply flowed through me. As a spiritual mystic I have the gift to hear and

Dr. Debra Ford Msc.D

as an inspirational teacher I have the gift of being able to communicate what I have heard. I chose the perfect SolePath in my plan to make the manifestation of SolePath possible.

In subsequent meditations I learned that SolePath is a gift from my non-physical guides, my council of seven. SolePath was made manifest because we are ready. SolePath was made manifest because it is time for us to gain clarity around the fundamental questions of life. SolePath was made manifest so that we can get on purpose and ask 'how may we serve' to make a difference to our world. SolePath was made manifest so that each of us can reach for the great truth that is within us.

Since 2009, working with John, the SolePath body of work has been developed and expanded. The sacred downloaded information includes the 22 LightPaths, 22 DarkPaths and 6 categories. SolePath is a body of work that is growing and changing and the only constant is the sacred downloaded information for the LightPaths, DarkPaths and categories. I have left strict instructions for those who will continue the work after I go home, that all may be improved, edited, worked on − except this.

The writings for each of the 22 SolePaths are so multilayered, with so many levels of understanding that I think it could only have come from a non-physical source. All of us who work with these 22 LightPaths and DarkPaths daily, are constantly surprised by the new understandings that come each time we read the teachings.

The first reading brings an initial understanding; the second reading reaches into a different layer; the third reading goes even deeper; new understandings revealed as we are ready to hear and receive and integrate our gifts and greatness into our own lives.

We have been given guidance on how to accurately complete

a SolePath energy analysis using dowsing and carefully selecting and training those who have this extraordinary gift of connecting for this information. More on this in section three.

We have created a mentoring process that helps with understanding and integrating your personal SolePath into your life so that you can walk your unique path to a beautiful, meaningful life filled with purpose. More on this in section four.

What has felt important to me is to distinguish the work that is sacred. To know which part of the teaching is a work in progress that must change and stay current with the times, that must be relevant to the ages.

Most importantly, though, to know which part of the work must be allowed to stay still so that we never tamper with the words of spirit or the many layers of understanding that become apparent depending on where we are in our own lives.

What is SolePath

SolePath is who you were born to be. It is your guide to a beautiful life, filled with happiness, peace, joy, love, purpose and meaning. When you know your SolePath, you can navigate the pitfalls; those things that trip you up in your life, and connect with your unique, personal, individual gifts and greatness.

SOLEPATH IS A TEACHING THAT IS DIRECTIONAL — GIVING A FRAMEWORK TO AN EARTH INCARNATION. SOLEPATH PROVIDES A

Dr. Debra Ford Msc.D

SETH

Your SolePath is imprinted on your sub-conscious. Your behaviour, your attitudes and your beliefs are all a sub-conscious response to what is going on around you and this response to life is governed by your SolePath imprint. SolePath is the reason you behave the way that you do; it governs your behaviour and regulates your response to everything that impacts your life.

Your SolePath is a braid of two expanding LightPaths, a progression LightPath and a joyful LightPath, and one collapsing DarkPath.

YOU CHOOSE YOUR SOLEPATH BECAUSE IT PROVIDES THE PERFECT OPPORTUNITIES FOR YOU AS AN INDIVIDUAL TO EXPERIENCE YOUR INCARNATION. YOU CHOOSE YOUR SOLEPATH TO EXPERIENCE YOUR GIFTS AND GREATNESS IN RELATIONSHIP WITH OTHERS.

SETH

LightPaths are a place of expanded energy and when you live your life from this place of expanded energy you find joy, health, love, happiness and meaning. Your LightPaths connect you with your gifts and greatness so that you can live with purpose and learn how you can serve to make a difference in the world. Reaching for your LightPaths and choosing away from your DarkPath is how you have the life experience your soul intended.

Your DarkPath is a place of collapsed energy, and harbours the skills that cause your energetic collapse. When you live your life from this place of collapsed energy, life is a challenge.

THE SECRET TO A HAPPY LIFE ...THERE IS ONLY ONE WAY TO DO THIS ... TO CHOOSE A BETTER FEELING IN THE MOMENT. TO CHOOSE TO FEEL BETTER RIGHT HERE, RIGHT NOW. IT IS THE REASON FOR YOUR EXISTENCE. THIS IS THE PURPOSE OF YOUR LIFE. ALL ELSE FLOWS FROM THIS. IN EACH EXPERIENCE OF YOUR LIFE, AS YOU DETERMINE YOUR FEELINGS, TO MAKE CHOICES THAT CREATE A BETTER FEELING. THE ENERGETIC IMPACT OF THIS ON YOUR PLANET IS HUGE; THE IMPACT ON SELF IS HUGE; THE IMPACT ON COMMUNITY IS HUGE. AND SOLEPATH PROVIDES THE CLUES, THE DIRECTION FOR CHOOSING THAT BETTER FEELING. SIMPLE ISN'T IT?

SETH

Living in your LightPaths requires deliberate, conscious choice, a reaching for meaning, for a beautiful life. Your DarkPath is a place of familiarity, a behavioural tendency, a past life completion; been there, done that.

CHOOSE WELL. IT IS FUN. SOLEPATH PROVIDES THE CLARITY AROUND WHAT TO CHOOSE. IT IS TRUE THAT THERE IS EXPANDING BEHAVIOUR THAT ENCOMPASSES ALL AND THAT THIS WILL HAVE A HUGE IMPACT ON YOUR PLANET. IT IS FURTHER TRUE THAT EACH OF YOU NEEDS DIRECTION FOR CHOOSING. THIS IS WHY THE SOLEPATH TEACHING WAS BROUGHT INTO REALITY ON EARTH. WE ARE WISHING TO SPEED UP THE ENERGETIC SHIFT FOR 'ALL'. IT IS SIMPLY TIME FOR EACH OF YOU TO KNOW YOUR PLACE WITHIN THE COLLECTIVE, THE 'ALL'. FOR EACH OF YOU TO KNOW THE IMPACT YOU CAN HAVE ON THE GOODNESS FOR 'ALL'.

SETH

LightPaths are where you feel positive emotions, when you are in the flow and life just feels easier. This is the energy from which your great truth will emerge. Your DarkPath is

Dr. Debra Ford Msc.D

where you feel negative emotions, where you feel stuck and that life is difficult, as if you are struggling upstream.

THIS LIFE IS ONLY ABOUT JOY YOU KNOW. SOME LIVE LIVES OF JOY, NOT BECAUSE ONLY JOYFUL THINGS HAPPEN TO THEM BUT BECAUSE THEY ARE CAUTIOUS AND DELIBERATE ABOUT THEIR RESPONSE TO WHAT IS HAPPENING IN THEIR LIVES. CHOOSE JOY. PERHAPS TODAY YOU CAN CHOOSE TO FEEL SAFE. PERHAPS TODAY YOU CAN CHOOSE NOT TO RESIST. CHOOSE SOMETHING DIFFERENT, CHOOSE SOMETHING MORE POSITIVE; IT IS POSSIBLE. AND SOLEPATH PROVIDES THE DIRECTION FOR CHOOSING. WONDERFUL ISN'T IT? CONSCIOUSLY CHOOSING, DELIBERATELY CREATING A LIFE OF JOY.

SETH

When you live in your LightPaths and are living the life your soul intended, you are connected to your wisdom. You put yourself in a position to hear your higher self; to receive the inspiration from your guides, your angels, your god. Your gifts and greatness are in your LightPaths and they are the secret to manifesting your great truth.

WE HAVE USED MANY METAPHORS TO TRY TO GIVE YOU A VISUAL OF WHAT THIS NAVIGATION PIECE CALLED SOLEPATH MEANS. WE HAVE GIVEN THE VISUAL OF THE BANKS OF THE RIVER, WE HAVE USED THE CHOICES AND BEHAVIOUR WORDS. AND HERE IS WHAT WE ATTEMPT TO DO. IN EVERY MOMENT OF EVERY DAY YOU ARE FACED WITH CHOICES; YOU ARE FACED WITH LIGHT AND DARK CHOICES AND SOLEPATH IS THE NAVIGATION OF THAT. AND SO IN MOMENTS IN YOUR LIFE YOU WILL BE IN THE FLOW BETWEEN THE BANKS OF YOUR RIVER, IN MOMENTS OF YOUR LIFE YOU WILL STAND AT THE FORK IN YOUR ROAD, WHERE YOUR ONLY CHOICE IS, WHAT WOULD MY LIGHTPATHS DO HERE; WHAT WOULD MY DARKPATH DO HERE; AND THIS IS HOW YOU NAVIGATE THOSE MOMENTS.

SETH

SECTION 2 – SETH'S SOLEPATH TEACHINGS

- SolePath and your health
- Choices and behavior
- Seth's time tools
- Destiny versus free will

A NEW ENERGY IS UNFOLDING. YOU, SOULS ON EARTH AT THIS TIME, ARE THE PIONEERS. ALL IS WELL. MORE AND MORE WILL BEGIN TO ASK 'HOW MAY I SERVE?', THE ENERGY WILL MOVE FROM ME TO US, IT IS THE DESTINY OF YOUR PLANET.

SETH

Dr. Debra Ford Msc.D

SECTION 2 – SETH'S SOLEPATH TEACHINGS

Funnily enough I am not always keen to speak with Seth. Sometimes I just want to live in the grey areas and to not tie things down like my intellectual SolePath husband needs to. I really do sometimes want the intangible and inexplicable to remain that way, what else will my spiritual mystic have to think about on my walks?

Yet we have had some fun and enlightening conversations with Seth since he has been such an integral part of the development of the SolePath work. Seth has given us so much insight into life's bigger questions, such as why children get sick, destiny versus free will, our life's time tunnel, choosing the pictures on our wall.

Seth tells us repeatedly that he has an opinion on just about everything, and I can concur with that! Here is some of the wisdom he has shared and perhaps it can help as you move towards your own purpose and create your great truth.

SolePath and your health

Your LightPaths are the source of health, your mental, physical and metaphysical health. Your DarkPath is the cause of your mental and physical dis-ease and spiritual disconnection.

IT IS TRUE THAT THE CAUSE OF DISEASE IS THE PLACE OF COLLAPSED ENERGY THAT YOU CALL THE DARKPATH. AND THIS IS A TOOL FOR CHOOSING AWAY FROM ILLNESS; CHOOSING YOUR EXPANDED ENERGY YOUR LIGHTPATHS.

SETH

When you live your life in a place of expanded energy you protect yourself energetically. A normal healthy, energetic aura extends about six to eight feet out from your body. Your LightPath energy extends up to thirty feet out from your body, not only out in front of you but in a 360 circle around you, providing you with a powerful energetic shield.

Your DarkPath energy is a complete energetic implosion. When you respond to the world from your DarkPath you are vulnerable emotionally, mentally and physically. In this place of energetic collapse you get ill, whether it is serious illness or simply a quick pain in your neck. In this place of energetic collapse you experience negative thought and negative emotion, whether it be chronic depression or moments of stress. In this place of energetic collapse you are disconnected from your wisdom, your instincts, your common sense, your higher self, your soul, your guides, your god, your great truth.

SOLEPATH IS A KEY TO MENTAL, PHYSICAL AND SPIRITUAL HEALTH. BUT WE DO NOT WISH TO FACILITATE HEALING ONLY FOR THE SAKE OF THE INDIVIDUAL BUT ALSO FOR THE REASON THAT WHEN THE INDIVIDUAL IS HEALTHY THEY BEGIN TO MOVE THEIR FOCUS FROM 'I TO US'. THEY BEGIN TO PARTICIPATE IN COMMUNITY. SOLEPATH NOT ONLY PROVIDES THE CLUES TO HEALING BUT ALSO TO PURPOSE.

SETH

Seth has further teachings with regard to health and healing.

ILLNESS IS PART OF A LIFE INCARNATION, A VERY IMPORTANT PART OF A LIFE INCARNATION. IT IS IN A PLACE OF PHYSICAL VULNERABILITY THAT IMPORTANT LESSONS ARE LEARNED. ILLNESS MAY BE PART OF YOUR SOUL'S PLAN; THE EXPERIENCE OF IT, THE CHOOSING TOWARDS

Dr. Debra Ford Msc.D

HEALTH OR THE CHOOSING AWAY FROM HEALTH.

When children are ill with chronic illness it is certainly part of their plan and the plan of those who care for them. 'Who will I be' in relation to this young child and their experience of illness.

When adults have chronic illness it could be part of their plan, or it could be a creation of their life, the way they have lived their life. All illnesses have a metaphysical meaning and you create the whole experience, not only the disease but also the life experiences that create the disease.

It is true that you are creating illness with your negative thought. What is missing from this teaching, the part that creates the feeling of somehow being imperfect and wrong, is the plan. You cannot know from your physical incarnation all of the aspects of your soul plan. But you can evolve through experience; you can evolve through choosing away from what you do not want. You are on earth to experience contrast and illness is contrast, it is what you do not want.

You are perfect creators and in writing illness into your plan, you also wrote in all the tools and opportunities to choose health and wellbeing. This is the experience; choosing healthy habits, choosing healthy environments, choosing healers, choosing health.

Illnesses have many reasons. Sometimes just for pause, to take a moment for self to pause and to reconsider, for the universal plan to have a moment to unfold. It is in these moments of pause that magnificence is created.

These times of illness allow time to stand still. Sometimes for the experience with the outcome of humility, being humble about the experience of life and of others. Or an outcome of gratitude, being thankful for what you may be

TAKING FOR GRANTED. OR AN OUTCOME OF COMMUNITY, ALLOWING OTHERS TO TAKE CARE OF YOU AND FINDING COMFORT IN THIS.

YOU ARE HERD ANIMALS, YOU DO NEED EACH OTHER.

SETH

Choices and behaviour

SolePath is who you were born to be. It is your guide to a beautiful life, filled with happiness, peace, joy, love, purpose, meaning. When you know your SolePath, you can navigate the pitfalls; those things that trip you up in your life, and connect with your unique, personal, individual gifts and greatness.

Knowing your LightPaths and your DarkPath provides you with the path to purpose, the path to your great truth. In every moment, with every experience, interacting with others, you have a choice of how you will respond. Will you choose to live your LightPaths or your DarkPath and what are the consequences of that choice?

CHOOSING BEHAVIOUR. IT IS NOT THAT IT IS DIFFICULT TO CHOOSE BUT RATHER THAN YOU HAVE NOT BEEN AWARE THAT YOUR BEHAVIOUR IS A CHOICE. THERE IS AN ACCEPTANCE OF NEGATIVE AND WITHHOLDING BEHAVIOURS AND A SENSE THAT THEY HAPPENED WITHOUT PERSONAL PARTICIPATION.

YOU HAVE BECOME SO FOCUSED ON ME AND ON I. YOU SAY, I CAN'T HELP MY BEHAVIOUR, THAT PERSON MADE ME FEEL ANGRY, THAT PERSON CAUSED THIS, THAT PERSON IS RESPONSIBLE FOR MY ACTIONS. IN NOT CHOOSING YOUR LIGHT YOUR IMPACT ON THE 'WE' AND 'US' IS DEVASTATING. YOU SEE, BEHAVIOUR HAS THE GREATEST IMPACT ON THE 'WE' AND 'US'.

Dr. Debra Ford Msc.D

When you say that this other person caused my negative thought or feeling, you are actually saying that I have forgotten that I have a choice around this. They caused this and therefore are responsible for my behaviour. Therefore my negative impact on 'we' and 'us' is not because of me. I forgot that I had a choice

In every moment of every day, in every situation you are faced with choices. All of these choices have an outcome, or behaviour. This is one of the fundamental questions 'who will I be in relation to what is going on around me?' Every thought, feeling, action is a choice.

A situation arises that triggers a thought and emotion. You become aware of your thought and emotion and choose to hold onto that or not. In the moment of your awareness, you participate in choosing. When you deliberately choose withholding thought and emotion, you are deliberately steering yourself toward negative behaviour. This negative behaviour will always have a poor effect on someone else, maybe not in the moment, but at some time.

You speak of choosing out of negative behaviour and today it takes an hour before you choose better thoughts, feelings and actions. Next time you choose faster. As 'she' teaches this is indeed the way your soul evolves and yes, the path to enlightenment.

You have the free will to choose expanding behaviour and SolePath provides the clarity around what to choose. It is true that there is expanding behaviour that encompasses all and that this will have a huge impact on your planet. It is further true that each of you needs a direction for choosing. This is why the SolePath teaching was brought into reality on earth. We are wishing to speed up the energetic shift for all. It is simply time for each of you to know your place within the collective, the all. For each of

YOU TO KNOW THE IMPACT YOU CAN HAVE ON THE GOODNESS FOR ALL.

ALL IS WELL AND IF YOU AREN'T FEELING POSITIVE, JOYFUL, HAPPY, IT IS INCUMBENT ON YOU TO REACH FOR A BETTER FEELING. THIS IS YOUR ONLY ACTION, THIS MUST BE YOUR ONLY GOAL. ALL OF YOUR LIFE IS YOUR CREATION OR YOUR DESTINY; YOU ARE ONLY ON EARTH TO CHOOSE JOY AS YOU NAVIGATE THROUGH THESE EXPERIENCES. WE UNDERSTAND THE DIFFICULTY IN THIS, TRULY WE DO, AND YOU ARE ALL DOING SO WELL UNDER THE CIRCUMSTANCES. WE ARE WITH YOU, WITH ALL OF YOU, ALL OF THE TIME. CHOOSE JOY, MAKE A CONSCIOUS DELIBERATE CHOICE FOR JOY.

ONE CHOICE OF POSITIVE BEHAVIOUR, OF LOVING ACTIONS, HAS AN ENORMOUS IMPACT ON THE ALL. THIS IS THE SECRET TO YOUR INCARNATION, TO EACH OF YOU CHOOSING TO BE ON EARTH. AND CHOOSING IS MADE EASIER THROUGH KNOWING WHO YOU WERE BORN TO BE, THROUGH KNOWING THAT PART OF YOUR PLAN THAT YOU HAVE CALLED SOLEPATH. AND ALL OF THIS CAN ONLY BE DONE IN THE MOMENT, IN THE NOW.

SETH

In the previous quote, the 'she' that Seth refers to is me. He has only used my name once that I can recall. Others have these cute nicknames; he calls Deneen the butterfly, John the innovator, Terry the manager. Yes, he has a great sense of humour.

I have not yet developed the skill to speak with Seth directly myself. I can communicate in writing, writing down my questions and his answers, but I have not as yet had a direct verbal conversation with him as I do with Jane. When I speak as the voice of Seth, I am not really present during the sessions and don't remember much, if anything of what he says. I simply close my eyes and there he is, full of wisdom, sometimes kind, sometimes tough love, always focused on how he can motivate us to service.

Am I making it all up? Yes!

Is it all my imagination? Certainly! And sometimes, well most of the time, he has these simply brilliant ideas that neither I, nor anyone I know could have come up with. During Seth sessions with clients he sometimes raises really personal insights; it's almost as if he is weighing up the individual's response to him and choosing to throw in something that no one else would know about. He is fun, witty, warm and can be terribly disarming.

Seth's time tools

So when is the right time for you to start manifesting your great truth?

Now! It is truly all that you have. Being in the moment is the secret to happiness and fulfillment. Every moment is a new beginning.

SETH

Seth teaches that the secret to a happy life is to be present; to live in the moment and SolePath provides the navigation for each moment. Choosing your LightPaths right here, right now, to be present in expanding energy, that's a great place to start.

There is only one way to do this, to choose a better feeling, in the moment.

You are all called. If you do not use this moment, the now, this exact hour, minute, second to create positively, 'we' cannot be impacted in the way that earth and her inhabitants are ready. Choose to be content, satisfied, thankful for this very moment.

Truly thankful; particularly if the moment is unhappy. In this moment of unhappiness you experience an opportunity for choice. Who will you be?

There is a questioning, a questing that occurs in physical form that precludes you from living in the now. Many souls are waiting for something else, waiting for something better, waiting for anything that isn't this, what I am experiencing now. Now is all that you have. You are creative beings and it is only possible to create a future or an outcome from now.

The importance of this is greater and greater, as your planet supports the manifestation of thought more quickly. Being in a place of expanded energy in this moment is essential. Choosing, now, and being certain that all is well — that is your work.

SETH

So often in our lives we agonize over future outcomes, and the 'what if's'. We won't take the first step because we can't see the outcome.

We call Seth our breadcrumb guy — as he teaches us over and over again during our conversations with him that our only work is to make the best decision in the moment, to follow the next breadcrumb. He teaches us to ask what is my best move, right here, right now; this is how we create the most expanding future outcomes; this is how we create our positive future reality.

Moment by moment, an asking 'what is my next best step', this is the path to joy.

SETH

It seems so simple but it takes conscious deliberate effort not to try to make our choices all about future outcome, but to make the most expanding decision in the moment. Too many paths are intersecting, too many others are making choices, and ultimately, as Seth says over and over again, all is well and every outcome is a great outcome.

WE ARE OBSERVING A PREOCCUPATION WITH THOSE THINGS IN LIFE THAT BEAR NO REAL RELEVANCE TO WHAT LIFE IS ALL ABOUT. YOUR LIFE IS AN ILLUSION. WHY COULD IT NOT BE A POSITIVE, FUN AND JOYFUL ILLUSION? IN ALL TROUBLED OR DIFFICULT TIMES THE CHOICE OF A POSITIVE THOUGHT OR EMOTION IS THE ONLY WAY TO BEGIN. IT IS A LEARNED SKILL AND ONE THAT REQUIRES DELIBERATE INTENTION.

THIS IS A BIG PART OF WHY YOU CHOSE AN EARTH INCARNATION, THE EXPERIENCING OF CHOOSING A POSITIVE THOUGHT OR EMOTION AT CHALLENGING TIMES. YOU HAVE FORGOTTEN WHO YOU ARE; A PERFECT ETERNAL SOUL HAVING A PHYSICAL EXPERIENCE WITH THE ABSOLUTE AGREEMENT OF ALL OTHERS IN YOUR LIFE.

SETH

Seth speaks about the tunnel that our life is moving through and the pictures on the wall of our tunnel. In each moment we are making choices, looking at the pictures that guide the next moment and the one after that; choosing between pictures that represent our LightPaths and our DarkPath. I'm sure you have wondered what would have happened if ... you had taken that job overseas, you had married that other person ... you looked at certain pictures, you made life choices and here is where you have ended up.

When you created the plan for your life, you included all of the pictures on your tunnel wall, all of your choices, all of your life's possibilities. So you have never made any wrong choices, you have never looked at any incorrect pictures; they were all in your plan for the purpose of your soul's evolution.

Don't wish any part of your life away, especially the difficult times, you will miss the full importance of the experience, it is all part of your plan.

But right here, right now, what will you do, what will you choose from this moment, from this point of creation, from now?

Seth also teaches us that often the next best move is a pause. Taking a pause is so counter to what we think life is all about, we are so used to forcing and muscling things into submission. A pause allows the time for energy to line up, for things to shape up, for the best opportunities to become manifest and flow towards you. We are so unused to taking a pause in our lives and this is when illness shows up, literally forcing us to slow down or to stop.

STAY QUIET, STAY STILL, STAY PEACEFUL, ESCAPE, THIS IS OFTEN HOW TO CREATE THE BEST RESOLUTION. IN AN ENERGETIC PAUSE, YOU SEE SO MUCH BIRTH AS EVENTS ARE ALIGNED. STAY IN YOUR LIGHT, ALL IS WELL, LET GENTLENESS AND KINDNESS VIBRATE TOWARDS YOU.

SETH

Destiny versus free will

Of course, Seth loved entering this great debate, the destiny, free will, law of attraction debate; and he helped us make sense of it all and brought us a wonderful sense of relief.

There is a plan for our lives, a perfect plan created in conjunction with our soul community, for the express purpose of our perfect eternal soul's evolution. We write experiences and people into that plan and all of what we are

Dr. Debra Ford Msc.D

going through also benefits our entire soul community.

Our plan is our tunnel; you could almost say that our tunnel is our destiny. I am always going to be caucasian, female and born into my particular family, no matter how hard I wish, think or intend it to be different.

Choosing what pictures we will look at on the walls of our tunnel is our free will. Choosing to live in expanded energy, choosing to respond from our LightPaths and not our DarkPath, that is free will. In this way we create our life with our intentions, using the law of attraction and knowing what to choose, knowing what pictures to look at.

Yet, there are still events in our life that are going to test us; awful things can happen. And how will we grow through those experiences if we don't know if they are our destiny, written into our plan, or whether we caused them to happen by not choosing well using our free will?

When you have lived through something difficult, and done all of your personal growth work and there is still confusion around why it happened or how it happened, then this is probably part of your destiny. Just one of those experiences that either your soul wanted for personal experience, or you agreed to participate in with another soul for their experience.

Life happens, you have not willfully created all of your troubles, you are not to blame, and sometimes it was going to happen no matter what you did. Living a life that you are proud of doesn't mean that only good things will happen to you but it does mean that you can choose to experience what happens to you as a good thing. It's not what happens that is most important, it is how you respond that is key.

Seth encourages us to let things go and to focus on choosing light expanding behaviour, right here, right now. That is the next best move. Living in your LightPaths is never going to be the easiest path, but it is always going to be the most joyful. Living in your LightPaths is your direct connection to your soul and to your great truth.

SECTION 3 – SOLEPATH FOR YOU

- How your SolePath is analyzed
- The 22 SolePaths
- SolePath excerpts

For there is only one great adventure and that is inward towards self, for that, time nor space nor even deeds matter.
Tropic of Capricorn, Henry Miller

Dr. Debra Ford Msc.D

SECTION 3 – SOLEPATH FOR YOU

How your SolePath is analyzed

Learning how to discover a person's SolePath came from dowsing teachings that I had learnt years before SolePath was born. My study of feng shui at that time led me to dowsing buildings and land, curing negative energy to create spaces that nourish those who live and work there. All those years earlier I had learned this unique skill never dreaming that it would become part of the SolePath manifestation. It was one of my breadcrumbs.

Determining a person's SolePath is a mystical process and is completed by SolePath certified energy analysts chosen for their ability to connect metaphysically. Not surprisingly, we have found that only those individuals with spiritual SolePaths have the ability to accurately identify a SolePath on a consistent basis.

Photographs are used for the analysis to provide a very stable structural link to the field of energy. Some traditional religions don't allow the taking of personal photographs as they feel that each time an image is taken, a part of that person's soul is released. This is not our belief but it does emphasize the reason why we are able to use photographs when connecting to your SolePath, identifying the path, the navigation that your soul intended.

We have learned that each SolePath analysis can only be done once and therefore it must be done right, first time. In our process, just as in quantum mechanics, the way you look at things changes what you look at. The first look, correctly done, is always perfect. If a person is analyzed more than once, it is possible that they could get a different SolePath reading. The first analysis completed by a properly trained 'ath certified energy analyst is the correct analysis.

Every SolePath analysis is authenticated and approved by two analysts who work together. The first analyst completes the SolePath reading and the second analyst validates and verifies their connection to the field. The record is then filed in the SolePath institute library of records; an exclusive community of people who are striving to live with purpose.

SolePath energy analyses take place at the SolePath institute, a space that is energetically cleared and balanced to ensure unobstructed connection to the field. It's also an inspiring, comforting place for our analysts to complete their metaphysical work. Our analysts understand that delivering the correct SolePath to each individual is a sacred responsibility. We all take this very seriously.

The 22 SolePaths

Your SolePath is who you were born to be. It is your guide to a beautiful life, filled with happiness, peace, joy, love, purpose, meaning. When you know your SolePath, you can navigate the pitfalls; those things that trip you up in your life, and connect with your unique, personal, individual gifts and greatness.

WE ARE CONCERNED WITH THE PRIMARY REASON FOR EXISTENCE. EACH OF YOU MADE A DELIBERATE DECISION TO EXPERIENCE LIFE ON EARTH; EACH OF YOU CHOSE A DIFFERENT PATH; EACH OF YOU HAS GIFTS AND GREATNESS. WE WISH TO GUIDE YOU TO PURPOSE NOW; TO THE MANIFESTATION OF THOSE GIFTS AND GREATNESS INTO PURPOSE. ALL UNIQUE, ALL WITH SO MUCH TO OFFER; ALL WILLING TO SERVE AND TO HEAL YOUR PLANET.

WHEN EACH OF YOU CHOOSES LIGHT OR EXPANDING BEHAVIOUR — SOLEPATH PROVIDES DIRECTION. FOR ALL OF YOUR TALENTS ARE

NEEDED. ALL OF YOU CAME FOR A DIFFERENT WORK AND TO MAKE A DIFFERENT CONTRIBUTION; ALL CHOOSING YOUR LIGHT. THIS IS TRULY THE GIFT OF SOLEPATH, IDENTIFYING EACH PERSON'S OWN UNIQUE ABILITY TO MAKE A CONTRIBUTION.

SETH

There are 22 SolePaths, divided into 6 categories. Both your LightPaths and your DarkPath each belong to a category and these categories are group classifications, which are the overall guides to how you interact with the world.

The SolePath names sometimes cause misunderstanding. You may be an inspirational teacher like me and it doesn't mean that you need to stand in front of a classroom of children teaching day in and day out. You may be a dark compassionate healer like me and it doesn't mean that you can't help others; it just means that you will show up for your work differently. Letting go of the traditional meanings and delving into the sacred downloads is fun, interesting, enlightening and very important.

The charismatic category includes the adventurer, gladiator, influencer, leader and performer SolePaths.

The compassionate category includes the caretaker, facilitator and healer SolePaths.

The inspirational category includes the conformist, humanitarian, manager and teacher SolePaths.

The intellectual category includes the controller, expert and lateral thinker SolePaths.

The intuitive category includes the builder, creator, hunter and solitude SolePaths.

The spiritual category includes the balance, mystic and warrior SolePaths.

charismatic adventurer

spiritual balance

intuitive builder

compassionate caretaker

inspirational conformist

intellectual controller

intuitive creator

intellectual expert

compassionate facilitator

charismatic gladiator

compassionate healer

inspirational humanitarian

intuitive hunter

charismatic influencer

intellectual lateral thinker

charismatic leader

inspirational manager

spiritual mystic

charismatic performer

intuitive solitude

inspirational teacher

spiritual warrior

SolePaths – excerpts

The complete sacred downloaded SolePaths are included in Section 8. There is so much wisdom to absorb that sometimes an excerpt is a better first look, a bite sized, more manageable piece. Some of us have trouble recognizing our LightPaths and accepting that we are in fact marvelous! And that we all came to live a meaningful life and have important work to do.

I must confess that when downloading and writing the DarkPaths, I found myself really exhausted. We are here for growth and we are complicated beings; it was just tough writing it all down in one go, seeing it all, all of our dark, together, in one place.

Each of the 22 SolePaths manifests as light, expanded behaviour or as dark, collapsed behaviour. When living a SolePath as a DarkPath, it is a mastered skill, something we are very familiar with that has a 'been there done that' energy about it. When living a SolePath as a LightPath, it is often something that we have to reach a little harder for, something that might take us out of our comfort zone, and is ultimately so joyful, fulfilling and exciting.

The descriptions of the light and the dark for each category and for each SolePath within the category, are in the excerpts that follow.

Charismatic SolePaths

The five charismatic SolePaths are the adventurer, gladiator, influencer, leader and performer. These paths share overall charismatic characteristics and then have a very specific energy of their own.

Charismatic LightPaths

Charismatics are the world's 'sparkle' people. You simply light up our world. With your outgoing sensing and perception, just like a bat you are able to interpret the returning echoes from life. You respond to people, places and experiences by how you sense the world is responding to you. You use others as a mirror for yourself and have an innate sense of how people are reacting to you. You interpret the returning echoes and reflect back what you sense.

Your ability to judge situations keeps you safe because you are an incredible judge of character and you rarely make mistakes in your assessments. You get into difficulty when you don't trust this or allow the opinions of others to get in the way.

Charismatic DarkPaths

On the one hand, there is so much about being a charismatic that serves you — you are after all one of the world's 'sparkle' people — and on the other hand there is so much about being a dark charismatic that trips you up.

When you are living your charismatic category from a place of collapsed energy, the overall negative attitude is selfishness and a sense that it really is only about you.

You could easily delight us and light up our world, or use your big energy to shut out the light - even with the full knowing of what the impact is on those around you. You could use your incredible outgoing sensing and perception to amuse and enchant us, or to justify aggressive behaviour towards others.

Yet, when you are experiencing your charismatic category from a place of expanded energy, you contribute to our world with your sparkle, your light and your energy. You are fun and just make us all feel good.

Charismatic adventurer

LightPath

As a charismatic adventurer, you love the new and exciting - new learning, new people, new places, new technology ... anything new. You are a non-conformist and a ready – fire – aim person with an inexhaustible energy for life. You are a bit of a risk taker and are warm, affectionate and likeable.

Your core energy as a charismatic adventurer is:

loving the new and being at the cutting edge.

This core energy represents those positive core values deep within you that create an expansion of your energy; that create positive outcomes.

Being a charismatic adventurer means embracing the new. It means loving change and being discerning about when you are changing for the sake of change, or when you are embracing change because it is an improvement, a moving forward. You teach us how not to fear change and how to embrace new ideas. You show us that moving forward is fun and that the status quo can be improved upon.

DarkPath

The core energy for the dark charismatic adventurer is being a risktaker and gambler. Taking unnecessary risks, whatever the impact on others, whether it be for your safely, your health, in your selection of love partners, or even risking what others have.

Dr. Debra Ford Msc.D

Charismatic gladiator

LightPath

As a charismatic gladiator, you raise the bar; you push us to higher standards. You are motivated by competition and raise the standards of performance of all of us. You love excitement and are always on the look out for an opportunity to win. You have a deep belief in yourself and your innate skills.

Your core energy as a charismatic gladiator is:

excellence and raising the bar.

This core energy represents those positive core values deep within you that create an expansion of your energy; that create positive outcomes.

Being a charismatic gladiator means always striving for a better standard, pushing the rest of us to a higher standard of excellence, always raising the bar. You just want to be better and love a competitive environment. You just sense that it could be better!

DarkPath

The core energy for the dark charismatic gladiator is being ruthless and winning at all costs. Stretching the rules to get what you want, which is a win. Having a killer instinct and a deep feeling of superiority.

Charismatic influencer

LightPath

As a charismatic influencer, you influence us toward the greater good. You are an in charge person who is inspiring. You are believable and have the gift of the gab and are interested in and know and understand people. Your personal goals are for the greater good and you need to be independent.

Your core energy as a charismatic influencer is:

> encouraging collaboration and influencing for the greater good.

This core energy represents those positive core values deep within you that create an expansion of your energy; that create positive outcomes.

Being a charismatic influencer means that you understand how to get people to work with you to achieve your intentions. You are a great motivator when convincing others to work with you and you deeply understand collaboration.

DarkPath

The core energy for the dark charismatic influencer is manipulating to get what you want. Being self-centered and using others as pawns to achieve your own goals. Feeling that the rules don't apply to you.

Charismatic leader

LightPath

As a charismatic leader, you show others the way by your example. You are charismatic, believable and fun to be around. Your excitement about life is infectious. You understand people, their attitudes and motivation and have an incredible ability to think on your feet.

Your core energy as a charismatic leader is:

leading others and sparkle and charisma.

This core energy represents those positive core values deep within you that create an expansion of your energy; that create positive outcomes.

Being a charismatic leader means being born to lead – you simple gather a crowd. A bit like the movie character Forest Gump who decided to run and turned around to find that he had gathered a big following. They didn't know why he was running, or where he was going – but they simply felt drawn to follow him. That's a born leader.

DarkPath

The core energy for the dark charismatic leader is leading others astray. Feeling that it is their fault if they follow you and not really caring where they end up. Stretching the rules and not really thinking things through.

Charismatic performer

LightPath

As a charismatic performer, the world is your stage. You love the limelight and being recognized and admired for your talent. You really must have an audience and are spontaneous and fun loving. You love sensation and drama and have the great gift of living in the moment.

Your core energy as a charismatic performer is:

performing and entertaining and being an extrovert.

This core energy represents those positive core values deep within you that create an expansion of your energy; that create positive outcomes.

Being a charismatic performer means that you understand that your life is a movie and you have the ability to rewrite the script at any moment. You do love to be the lead actor and direct your supporting cast and entertain your audience. You are really fun to be around.

DarkPath

The core energy for the dark charismatic performer is being a selfish drama queen. Feeling that life is all about you, that you are the star of the show and creating drama wherever you go.

Compassionate SolePaths

The three compassionate SolePaths are the caretaker, facilitator and healer. These paths share overall compassionate characteristics and then have a very specific energy of their own.

Compassionate LightPaths

Compassionates are the 'love' SolePaths. You respond to the world through your heart feeling. As a compassionate, you can absolutely trust your heart and when you do trust your positive emotions, you can be certain of a good outcome, situation or decision.

Your heart keeps you safe because when you clearly identify whether you are feeling 'good' or 'bad' about someone or something, you don't make mistakes. You get into difficulty when you don't trust this, or allow the opinions of others to get in the way.

Compassionate DarkPaths

On the one hand, there is so much about being a compassionate that serves you – you are after all one of the world's most loving people, with a big heart – and on the other hand there is so much about being a dark compassionate that trips you up.

When you are experiencing your compassionate category from a place of collapsed energy, the overall negative attitude is a victim mentality. You give and give to others and then feel taken advantage of. You do not set boundaries and then complain of being taken for granted. People really don't know how to interact with you or where they stand with you.

You are not the best judge of character and often make mistakes with people, either of the heart, or in business dealings. Because of this, you are fearful that something will always go wrong and this fear is generally what causes things to go wrong.

Yet, when you are experiencing your compassionate category from a place of expanded energy, your love and your big heart just makes us feel wonderful.

Compassionate caretaker

LightPath

As a compassionate caretaker, you happily care for others and are sympathetic, helpful and co-operative. You love people and love to be liked. You are extremely reliable, highly co-operative and a great team player. You are trusted.

Your core energy as a compassionate caretaker is:

feeling compassion and loving people.

This core energy represents those positive core values deep within you that create an expansion of your energy; that create positive, loving feelings.

Being a compassionate caretaker means loving humanity, loving other people and loving yourself too. It means being gentle on others and yourself and participating in the world with compassion. The interaction that brings you the most joy and peace and a feeling of being on purpose, is connecting with people in a loving way.

DarkPath

The core energy for the dark compassionate caretaker is being a victim. Overreacting to perceived personal criticism and feeling that you never receive enough thanks.

Compassionate facilitator

LightPath

As a compassionate facilitator, you are all about community. Once you have enfolded others into your community, your joy comes from being of service to them. You love your community, your family and your cultural traditions. You are loyal to a fault and are a sincere and sympathetic person. You are also responsible, reliable and hard working. To be part of a facilitator's community and to be loved by a facilitator is a gift indeed!

Your core energy as a compassionate facilitator is:

desire to be of service and love of my community.

This core energy represents those positive core values deep within you that create an expansion of your energy; that create positive, loving feelings.

Being a compassionate facilitator means creating community wherever you go and loving and being of service to this community. It means participating in the lives of your community – your family and friends – and creating meaningful relationships. The interaction that brings you the most joy and peace and a feeling of being on purpose, is connecting with the people you love.

DarkPath

The core energy for the dark compassionate facilitator is having a 'sheep mentality'. Following blindly and being easily lead astray. Sometimes being a poor judge of character and then being unable to listen to reason when this is pointed out to you.

Dr. Debra Ford Msc.D

Compassionate healer

LightPath

As a compassionate healer, you care about all living things and have a deep desire to help alleviate pain and suffering and bring wholeness and health to the world. You know how to 'fix' what is broken in our world; once you have decided what it is that you would like to heal — you know how to take the steps to do this. You have a very clear sense of right and wrong, you follow your heart not your head and are willing to make sacrifices for what you believe in.

Your core energy as a compassionate healer is:

healing people, animals or the planet and fixing what is wrong.

This core energy represents those positive core values deep within you that create an expansion of your energy; that create positive, loving feelings.

Being a compassionate healer means choosing what it is that you would like to heal and then taking action towards that. What you 'fix' will be aligned with your personal beliefs and it could involve people, animals or our planet. The interaction that brings you the most joy and peace and a feeling of being on purpose, is connecting with all living things in a loving way.

DarkPath

The core energy for the dark compassionate healer is blaming yourself and feeling responsible for all of the bad things that happen around you. You feel constantly criticized and never feel good enough.

Inspirational SolePaths

The four inspirational SolePaths are the conformist, humanitarian, manager and teacher. These paths share overall inspirational characteristics and then have a very specific energy of their own.

Inspirational LightPaths

Inspirationals are the world's role models. You respond to the world by wanting to fill a perceived need. As an inspirational, you ask, "What does the world need and how can I provide it?" and "What do you need, and how can I help?"

You have an innate sense of responsibility to yourself, to others and to community, and look at what is needed by both individuals and the group at large. Inspirational SolePaths have the same role as the bones of the body; you provide the structure, the skeleton, the framework for society.

This does not mean that your own needs are lost in your desire to serve, but rather that through your personal learning and experience you feel great empathy with the needs of others and then take action. You inspire us by the way you live your own life and have a great capacity for getting things done to help others.

Inspirational DarkPaths

On the one hand, there is so much about being an inspirational that serves you — you are after all one of the world's role models — and on the other hand there is so much about being a dark inspirational that trips you up.

When you are experiencing your inspirational category from a place of collapsed energy, the overall negative attitude is entitlement and a demand that others obey you. You feel that you are the only one who sees what the world needs and you are certain that your opinions are the only ones that are right. (Even you can see that this is not possible.)

You are intolerant and demand that others look up to you and in the same breath, when you aren't obeyed, complain that you get no support. It must be a throw over from a past life when others were compelled to obey you. Seriously!

Yet, when you are experiencing your inspirational category from a place of expanded energy, you are pretty amazing as you have this deep desire to work towards making a difference in the world.

Inspirational conformist

LightPath

As an inspirational conformist the greatest gift that you share with us is your ability to build on what has gone before. Whether it is physical or metaphysical, you have this uncanny ability to see what has gone wrong and what has been extraordinary. You help us create more of what is positive and good, while not repeating the errors of the past and you make sure that the benefits of time honoured traditions are not lost. You have a great sense of right and wrong, are a dependable straight talker who is down to earth and responsible.

Your core energy as an inspirational conformist is:

valuing tradition and cultivating order.

This core energy represents those positive core values deep within you that create an expansion of your energy; that create inspiring outcomes.

Being an inspirational conformist means building on what has gone before, not losing what has been great about the past, not rejecting proven traditions. You really understand 'not throwing the baby out with the bath water' and are able to see what has worked before and what will provide a firm foundation for the future.

DarkPath

The core energy for the dark inspirational conformist is being hard hearted. Having an intolerant attitude when demanding that others conform to your paradigm; being closed to new ideas; and lacking in emotion.

Dr. Debra Ford Msc.D

Inspirational humanitarian

LightPath

As an inspirational humanitarian the greatest gift that you share with us is your desire to work for the greater good of all. You work tirelessly for the collective good, righting wrongs. You have a great depth of talent and courage and are a team player when working for a cause that meets your personal beliefs. You have a strong sense of duty and responsibility.

Your core energy as an inspirational humanitarian is:

fulfilling my duty and taking action.

This core energy represents those positive core values deep within you that create an expansion of your energy; that create inspiring outcomes.

Being an inspirational humanitarian means finding a cause and then putting a great deal of effort and time into making a difference. You are an active doer who needs to be getting things done, not sitting around talking about what needs to be done.

DarkPath

The core energy for the dark inspirational humanitarian is neglecting those closest to you. Neglecting your personal life and those you love; feeling that the rights of humanity are more important than the rights of the individual.

Inspirational manager

LightPath

As an inspirational manager the greatest gift that you share with us is your extraordinary ability to get things done. You make and implement plans and are a great organizer, supervisor, delegator and participant. You are very competent and proud of your abilities; a little strong willed and always on the go. You really know how to move things forward.

Your core energy as an inspirational manager is:

implementation and accomplishment.

This core energy represents those positive core values deep within you that create an expansion of your energy; that create inspiring outcomes.

Being an inspirational manager means inspiring people and managing projects. You understand that people can't be managed but need to be inspired to get things moving forward.

DarkPath

The core energy for the dark inspirational manager is being a perfectionist. Lacking a belief in others. Being strong willed, dictatorial, intolerant and demanding. Noticing the negative.

Dr. Debra Ford Msc.D

Inspirational teacher

LightPath

As an inspirational teacher your greatest gift is your ability to communicate so that others can understand. You look for the best in everyone and can find the talent in everyone. You are interested in people and connect in a way that is inspiring, warm, outgoing and enthusiastic.

Your core energy as an inspirational teacher is:

talented communicator and inspiring life.

This core energy represents those positive core values deep within you that create an expansion of your energy; that create inspiring outcomes.

Being an inspirational teacher means helping others to understand. Teachers are the world's great communicators, however you choose to do this - speaking, writing and by the way you live your life.

DarkPath

The core energy for the dark inspirational teacher is diminishing and hurting others. Being dismissive, choosing favourites and ostracizing others; being inflexible.

Intellectual SolePaths

The three intellectual SolePaths are the controller, expert and lateral thinker. These paths share overall intellectual characteristics and then have a very specific energy of their own.

Intellectual LightPaths

Intellectuals are the great minds of our world. You respond to the world with logical thought and considerable intelligence. It may be likely that our traditional school system has let you down, so you may not really understand your great mental capacity.

You can trust your ability to think things through and your thought processes are very reliable. There really isn't anything you can't solve when you give yourself enough time and put your mind to it. Your mind points you in the right direction because when you clearly think things through you always know what to do. You get into difficulty when you don't trust this, or allow the opinions of others to get in the way.

Intellectual DarkPaths

On the one hand, there is so much about being an intellectual that serves you — you are after all one of the world's great minds — and on the other hand there is so much about being a dark intellectual that trips you up.

When you are experiencing your intellectual category from a place of collapsed energy, the overall negative attitude is arrogance and a feeling that everyone else is an idiot. You think that you are the only one who is right and you don't mind making others feel stupid. You use your considerable intellect to tear down and criticize rather than to build up and create. Pity isn't it?

You are good with words and instead of using language to make others feel good, you often take on a condescending tone. It takes you a while to realize that saying the same thing, but in a louder more irritated voice, doesn't usually make what you are saying easier to understand. Seriously!

Yet, when you are experiencing your intellectual category from a place of expanded energy, you contribute to our world with your considerable intellect and your amazing ability to think things through.

Intellectual controller

LightPath

As an intellectual controller you are a visionary. You have a strong natural urge to establish structure and give direction in all situations; to create the plan, to set the rules. As a visionary you love to take on responsibility and are a great organizer and coordinator. You are confident and have a great belief in self.

Your core energy as an intellectual controller is:

vision to see the future and establishing structure.

This core energy represents those positive core values deep within you that create an expansion of your energy; that create thoughtful outcomes.

Being an intellectual controller means that you thrive when you are intellectually stimulated. You are mainly interested in people and information that are relevant to your future projects. You need a quiet focused environment so that you can logically focus on the task or subject at hand (no background music, side conversations or other distractions).

DarkPath

The core energy for the dark intellectual controller is seeking revenge. Blaming others, acting in a restrictive, dictatorial, authoritarian and insensitive manner.

Dr. Debra Ford Msc.D

Intellectual expert

LightPath

As an intellectual expert you are a specialist. You acquire extensive knowledge that provides clarity and understanding to others. You are highly skilled and insightful in your field and work well alone. You like expert status and recognition, and why not, you have done the work, the study and the research.

Your core energy as an intellectual expert is:

desire to acquire knowledge and specialization in one or two fields.

This core energy represents those positive core values deep within you that create an expansion of your energy; that create thoughtful outcomes.

Being an intellectual expert means that you thrive on having intimate knowledge of your chosen field of interest. You never skim the surface but rather spend your time researching and specializing in the one or two topics that captivate you. The image is of a pyramid or triangle above your head, distilling the ideas and thoughts that flow from your research and learning into a peak of specialization.

DarkPath

The core energy for the dark intellectual expert is thinking that you can never be nor do enough; being dissatisfied with your achievements. Constantly seeking approval and thinking that you are always lacking.

Intellectual lateral thinker

LightPath

As an intellectual lateral thinker you think outside the box. You follow the 180 rule, which is to turn around and look at things from a completely different direction. In this way you are able to encourage new and different ideas. You are an interesting conversationalist who is mentally quick and loves change. You are excited about life and easily acquire new skills.

Your core energy as an intellectual lateral thinker is:

innovative thinking and original ideas.

This core energy represents those positive core values deep within you that create an expansion of your energy; that create thoughtful outcomes.

Being an intellectual lateral thinker means that you thrive on different ideas. You are captivated by interesting concepts and engaging interaction and conversation with others. The image is of an upside down triangle or funnel above your head, capturing all of the ideas and thoughts that flow into your mind.

DarkPath

The core energy for the dark intellectual lateral thinker is being arrogant about your intellect. Having a superior attitude when dealing with others and making them feel uncertain.

Dr. Debra Ford Msc.D

Intuitive SolePaths

The four intuitive SolePaths are the builder, creator, hunter and solitude. These paths share overall intuitive characteristics and then have a very specific energy of their own.

Intuitive LightPaths

Intuitives are the 'gut' reaction SolePaths. You respond to the world through your body. As an intuitive, it is important to identify your body's responses; to know whether a particular sensation means go or stop.

Your body keeps you safe with its immediate reaction to people, situations and experiences. Sometimes it is a feeling in the pit of your stomach, or it may be tingling or goose bumps. When you clearly identify whether the physical sensation you are feeling is 'good' or 'bad' about someone or something, you don't make mistakes. You get into difficulty when you don't trust this, or allow the opinions of others to get in the way.

Intuitive DarkPaths

On the one hand, there is so much about being an intuitive that serves you — you are after all one of those who can recognize and understand your body and gut reaction to the world — and on the other hand there is so much about being a dark intuitive that trips you up.

When you are experiencing your intuitive category from a place of collapsed energy, the overall negative attitude is sabotage. You simply won't trust your own wisdom and your gut and you allow the opinions of others to get in the way. You think that you don't know anything, that everyone else knows better than you and that you always make the wrong decisions. Weird isn't it that you would not listen to your most reliable guide – yourself!

You really do know what is best for you, yet sometimes it seems that you deliberately go out to sabotage your success – wherever it may be, in relationships, at work, anywhere in your life. Stop it!

Yet, when you are experiencing your intuitive category from a place of expanded energy, your guidance is so certain, so reliable and so accurate.

Intuitive builder

LightPath

As an intuitive builder, you are a practical ideas person. You have an extraordinary ability to see the possibilities, to know the end result and how everything fits together. You form things into something better, you organize and connect. You make things happen. You are a tireless ideas person who is also emotional.

Your core energy as an intuitive builder is:

seeing possibilities and creating abundance.

This core energy represents those positive core values deep within you that create an expansion of your energy; that create positive knowing.

Being an intuitive builder means finding ways to manifest your ideas and networking and connecting people for shared opportunities. It means understanding that you are an emotional yet loving person who is always on the look out for the next building block; the next piece of your puzzle. Your greatest fulfillment in seeing your ideas become reality is sharing the abundance of wealth and happiness with others.

DarkPath

The core energy for the dark intuitive builder is dark, uncaring mood swings. Making too much of being a deep complex person and generally feeling discontented with life.

Intuitive creator

LightPath

As an intuitive creator, you are a beautiful ideas person. Your beautiful ideas may manifest as physical things, or may be beautiful conversations, beautiful interactions with others or beautiful experiences. You have an extraordinary ability to manifest original, beautiful creations. Your actions speak louder than your words and you are a sensitive, sometimes serious, naturally reserved and quiet person. You have a strong set of values and pursue your own unique goals.

Your core energy as an intuitive creator is:

creating beauty and manifesting ideas.

This core energy represents those positive core values deep within you that create an expansion of your energy; that create positive knowing.

Being an intuitive creator means finding ways to make our world more beautiful; your life's purpose is to leave our world more beautiful. Your very presence makes the world more beautiful and you have an uncanny ability to explore and share ideas that leave others feeling more beautiful. There is no limit to your creative ideas that include beautiful personal style, beautiful spaces and environments, beautiful experiences. Your greatest fulfillment is creating beauty in the world.

DarkPath

The core energy for the dark intuitive creator is dissatisfaction. Being chronically dissatisfied with your life and acting in an uncompromising and unfeeling manner.

Dr. Debra Ford Msc.D

Intuitive hunter

LightPath

As an intuitive hunter, you are a truth seeker. You are curious, enquiring and have a thirst for answers and understanding. Once you have found your 'truth' you love to share this knowledge with your community. You are a courageous person who is hard driving and brave, yet also thoughtful and considerate of others. You love the outdoors.

Your core energy as an intuitive hunter is:

seeking truth and answers and generosity.

This core energy represents those positive core values deep within you that create an expansion of your energy; that create positive knowing.

Being an intuitive hunter means always seeking. Your life flows much like the traditional hunter who was responsible for feeding community. With your courage and bravery you hunt the truth and then return to share this with your community. Because of the energy expended you then need time to sit by the fireside to rejuvenate and it is very important to take time for this rest. Your greatest fulfillment is finding truth to share with others.

DarkPath

The core energy for the dark intuitive hunter is being unmotivated; living and working in 'spurts' and feeling entitled to be lazy and selfish. Not valuing possessions, your own or those that belong to others.

Intuitive solitude

LightPath

As an intuitive solitude, you have a great imagination and require quiet to manifest your ideas. You are very comfortable and content when you are alone and able to be yourself. You may be a little unconventional and even a little eccentric; you certainly are independent and introspective and are very self motivated.

Your core energy as an intuitive solitude is:

imagination, quietness and contentment.

This core energy represents those positive core values deep within you that create an expansion of your energy; that create positive knowing.

Being an intuitive solitude means that much like Beatrix Potter, you love to retreat into quiet so that you can express and manifest your imagination; and then return to peaceful and loving interactions with others. Your greatest fulfillment is manifesting your imaginative ideas.

DarkPath

The core energy for the dark intuitive solitude is being introverted, antisocial and emotionally unavailable. Sometimes holding grudges for years.

Dr. Debra Ford Msc.D

Spiritual SolePaths

The three spiritual SolePaths are the balance, mystic and warrior. These paths share overall spiritual characteristics and then have a very specific energy of their own.

Spiritual LightPaths

Spirituals' life experience is exploring beliefs and 'what others cannot see' from this physical perspective. To do this, spirituals need to make time to nourish their spiritual connection through meditation and prayer. As a spiritual SolePath you push the boundaries of metaphysical beliefs, much like the intellectual SolePaths push the boundaries of logic and knowledge.

As a Spiritual, you can trust your connection. Because you are a spiritual explorer, your beliefs will change over the course of your lifetime. You enjoy the exploration of existing religious and spiritual beliefs as you create your own ideas around faith and the meaning of life.

Spiritual DarkPaths

On the one hand, there is so much about being a spiritual that serves you — you are, after all, one of the people most connected to non-physical energy — and on the other hand there is so much about being a dark spiritual that trips you up.

When you are experiencing your spiritual category from a place of collapsed energy, the overall negative attitude is superiority. You are dogmatic about your own beliefs and completely unaccepting about the beliefs of others. Not only do you feel that your beliefs are the only ones that are right, you are unwilling to look at another's perspective. It doesn't matter whether your beliefs are fundamental religion or the most liberal spirituality — your way is the right way.

You are a judgmental observer, standing on the sidelines of life, not participating yet judging others as wrong. It would be great fun for you to get in the game. Really!

Yet, when you are experiencing your spiritual category from a place of expanded energy, you contribute to our world with your spiritual exploring, you make it okay for us to believe in something 'bigger than ourselves', you push the boundaries of belief.

Dr. Debra Ford Msc.D

Spiritual balance

LightPath

As a spiritual balance, your gift to the world is showing us how to go with the flow. Your ability to create balance in your own life inspires us to find balance too. You are dependable, stable and love harmony. You have a genuine love of people and are warm, friendly, kind-hearted and generous.

Your core energy as a spiritual balance is:

going with the flow and living with grace.

This core energy represents those positive core values deep within you that create an expansion of your energy; that create positive, connected feelings.

Being a spiritual balance means flowing downstream and not resisting the flow of life. You love harmony and positive environments and know how to create those for yourself and for others. You understand that life can be simple when distractions are eliminated and we are all flowing downstream.

DarkPath

The core energy for the dark spiritual balance is being unable to make a decision. You don't commit to anything or anyone and have no remorse for letting others down. Trying to get a decision out of a dark balance is like trying to grab a handful of water.

Spiritual mystic

LightPath

As a spiritual mystic, your gift to the world is your spiritual exploration, actively elevating humanities' spiritual energy. You are connected to Source Energy and to your Higher Self. You have a talent for the written and spoken word and can communicate your spiritual experiences. You have a deep need for solitude and quiet private time.

Your core energy as a spiritual mystic is:

spirituality and connection.

This core energy represents those positive core values deep within you that create an expansion of your energy; that create positive, connected feelings.

Being a spiritual mystic means exploring the religious and spiritual beliefs of others and then deciding what you will believe in. Being a spiritual mystic means making spiritual exploration acceptable to others. Being a spiritual mystic means sharing your findings, new understandings and mystical experiences with others. Being a spiritual mystic means understanding that your beliefs will change over the course of your lifetime.

DarkPath

The core energy for the dark spiritual mystic is being judgmental, superior and arrogant. You are intolerant and unwilling to accept the beliefs of others and are dogmatic about your own beliefs.

Dr. Debra Ford Msc.D

Spiritual warrior

LightPath

As a spiritual warrior, your gift to the world is dedication to your spiritual cause. You hold deep convictions and will stand up for what you believe in. You are deeply connected and the only truly psychic SolePath. You have great integrity and can be counted on. You are capable and organized and have a tremendous amount of energy when working for your cause and what you believe in.

Your core energy as a spiritual warrior is:

integrity and dedication and psychic ability.

This core energy represents those positive core values deep within you that create an expansion of your energy; that create positive, connected feelings.

Being a spiritual warrior means that you are the spiritual SolePath with attitude; you are the mystic with sharp elbows. Your cause will change over the course of your lifetime and when you choose where to put your energy and effort, you are tireless.

DarkPath

The core energy for the dark spiritual warrior is being uncompromising. You are impatient and unfeeling and can walk over others; you won't allow anything to get in your way.

As I mentioned these are the SolePath excerpts. I have included the complete sacred downloaded SolePaths in Section 8. All of the paths sound so different, so great. Each of us with a different part to play in the energetic change that is occurring on our planet.

Your personal, unique SolePath provides the gifts for you to manifest your great truth. When you live your life in your LightPaths you have a direct connection to your soul, your higher self, you guides, your god — and this is where your great truth, your very unique teaching and contribution is waiting.

SECTION 4 – SOLEPATH INSIGHTS

- Understanding your SolePath
- SolePath key factors
- SolePath community
- SolePath daily ritual
- What SolePath has meant for others

SolePath is not a belief system. It is simply the way for you to navigate your life; the experiences, the people, the joy and the difficulties.

Dr. Debra

SECTION 4 – SOLEPATH INSIGHTS

It was all very well to have received the sacred SolePath download but what to do next, was the question. How to share this with others so that they could gain clarity around their gifts and greatness, and around what it is that is collapsing and holding them back in their lives.

This is what John and I have worked on together since 2009, bringing his charismatic intellectual and my inspirational spiritual gifts together.

It was a great learning for us and an unexpected experience as we realized that the SolePath body of work is organic, shifting and growing. We grew to understand that new inspiration received from so many sources, at different stages in the development of the work, brought new layers and depth to the teachings.

Within your body of work, within your great truth, discover what is fixed or sacred; what is changing and flowing and then allow the new insights to come in.

Listening to what others had to say was a big part of the creation of SolePath. As you manifest your great truth, talk about it, get feedback on it, have others take a look at what you are doing. But this comes with a capital b.u.t. Always trust yourself first; use your own personal navigation from your LightPaths to ensure the purity of your work. No one knows it better than you; no one lives it each and every day like you.

Feel thankful that your work will never be complete. As the energy of the world and those you are serving changes, so your great truth must evolve.

Understanding your SolePath

When you know your SolePath, when you know who you were born to be, it is a huge step towards a meaningful life; towards your life's purpose; towards living the life your soul intended.

SolePath is a daily awareness and a lifelong journey that guides you to 'how may I serve' and to manifesting your great truth.

LightPaths certainly challenge our limited view of self. Our SolePath certified mentors do the most wonderful work spending all day, every day, reminding people of how amazing they really are. It's a great job!

When reviewing the LightPaths we work with choices. What choices have you made in your life? What choices do you have? Have these choices brought you joy, love, happiness?

We also work on rewards. What rewards do you receive when living in your LightPaths? How you can allow more of this into your life? How you can get better at living in your LightPaths?

We also look at the gifts of the LightPaths. What talents are you not acknowledging? What is right about you that you are refusing to allow? How might accepting and using these gifts change your reality?

In the SolePath mentoring process we really focus on making the connection with all of the gifts and greatness of the LightPaths. But it is different for the DarkPath.

The DarkPath is the place of personal growth. It is what you are choosing away from. When we work with the DarkPath we review choices and behaviour. How to become more aware of

Dr. Debra Ford Msc.D

when you are responding to life from your DarkPath. How to choose away faster. How to evaluate the impact of your DarkPath choices and behaviour and how to get more of what you do want in your life.

We created a mentoring process, focus workbooks one to nine, that carefully walk clients through the integration of their SolePath into their life, while providing great tools, everyday practical actions that can be taken to help with living a life in expanded energy.

Thankfully, one of the ways to determine whether you are responding to people, experiences and other parts of your life from your LightPaths or DarkPath is really simple. Just take a moment to identify your emotions. Any positive emotion, under any circumstances, means you are living in your expanding energy or LightPaths. Any negative emotion and you are responding to the situation from your DarkPath.

It doesn't matter what your emotion is. Simply put, positive emotion equals LightPaths. Negative emotion equals DarkPaths. To quote Seth, 'simple isn't it?'

Take a look at the emotion zones chart on the next page.

Emotion zones

LightPaths	LightPaths
Active positive emotions	Passive positive emotions
Feeling happy, loving, joyful, cheerful, playful, bright, delighted, thankful, dynamic, eager, inspired, excited, enthusiastic, bold	Feeling content, safe, peaceful, satisfied, comfortable, relaxed, serene, free, certain, optimistic, confident, hopeful, calm, blessed
above	above
below	below
DarkPath	DarkPath
Active negative emotions	Passive negative emotions
Feeling angry, in despair, sulky, frustrated, wronged, frightened, worried, fearful, suspicious, panicked, threatened, offended, afflicted, bullying	Feeling victimized, depressed, powerless, ashamed, disappointed, discouraged, dissatisfied, lost, nervous, timid, doubtful, wary, rejected, injured

Above the line is experiencing life from your LightPaths; choosing positive emotion; living the life your soul intended; growing through your life experience; evolving as a human being and as a perfect eternal soul. This is where all of the joy, love, health, abundance, happiness lives.

Below the line is, experiencing life from your DarkPath; choosing negative emotion; well, you get the picture.

SolePath key factors

One of our challenges has been making the big concept of SolePath, the LightPaths and DarkPath, understandable and usable in everyday life.

We found that sometimes the information contained in the sacred downloaded SolePaths was just too much to process at one time. Some found it difficult to know where or how to begin integrating this into their life and this led us to create a way to identify priorities that we call the SolePath key factors.

We stress that learning to live in the LightPaths and reaching away from the DarkPath is a lifelong journey. Understandings about who you are and what is expanding for you and what trips you up, shows up as you live your day-to-day life; as you experience your life. It is not an instantaneous awakening, you have to live it, you have to experience it.

With SolePath key factors, a further energetic measuring, we are able to provide a point of focus, for right here, right now.

As you consider your great truth, find ways of allowing a gentle integration of your teachings. Take account of the fact that we are all at different stages in our personal growth and our spiritual development. Find ways to provide a focus, a starting point, a next step, the next breadcrumb, for those who are drawn to your work.

Here's how we did it. We can identify key success and failure priorities unique to each individual; specifically for this present moment (right here, right now); no more than three priorities at a time. This key factor identification allows a manageable integration, a reprogramming, a life lived in the LightPaths to begin.

SolePath Key Success Factors

SolePath key success factors are those personal characteristics that are fundamental to personal happiness and joy; right here, right now. Characteristics to focus on now as you integrate your extraordinary expanding LightPaths into your life; characteristics that provide clarity as you navigate to your life's purpose.

Remember, LightPaths are a place of expanded energy where your gifts and greatness lie. When you live your life from this place of expanded energy you find joy, health, love and happiness.

SolePath key success factors are a focus in your LightPaths at this point in your life and will probably change every twelve months or so. As you grow and evolve, your SolePath key success factors will give you an updated focus for personal growth.

I feel like knowing my key success factors is a good way to channel my energy and understand the skills/attributes that will allow me to be 'my best self'. I trust that the rest will come. If I can focus on my key success factors, for me, this will be easier than focusing on my life's purpose, which seems like an overwhelmingly huge undertaking.

Julian, intellectual controller and inspirational teacher

By having my key success factors identified from within my LightPath characteristics, it creates a fine-tuned focus from which to work from on a daily basis to remind myself of who I am (like a mantra) and how to strive for living in my LightPath, as well as gives encouragement and confirmation that I am moving in the right direction and can trust my intuition.

Karen, intuitive hunter and spiritual warrior

Dr. Debra Ford Msc.D

SolePath Key Failure Factors

SolePath key failure factors are personal characteristics that create pitfalls and undermine personal happiness; right here, right now. Behaviours and attitudes that keep you from living your life of joy; characteristics that when you deal with them allow you to navigate away from your dark collapsing energy, your dark thoughts and emotions.

Remember, the DarkPath is a place of collapsed energy, a mastered skill that provides choice points for personal growth. When you live your life from this place of collapsed energy, life is a challenge.

SolePath key failure factors are a focus in your DarkPath, top priorities and pitfalls that get in the way of your personal happiness and joy. As you work on these priorities, they too will change and are wonderful proof positive of your personal growth.

The awareness of what I need to focus on gives me guidance. Even if I respond from my darkness I am aware and at the very least say, next time the situation presents itself I will respond differently. I have learned that each situation that I am being presented with is for me to make a choice. 'How do I wish to respond?' If I respond from my dark energy the situation or circumstance will occur in a different way. If I choose my lightness, the situation is neutralized and I continue to learn and evolve. The learning continues until I choose light over dark, peace over chaos. Knowing this gives me hope that the joy filled path I am meant to live is here waiting for me!

Shirley, inspirational teacher and spiritual balance

Knowing my SolePath has been enlightening, and knowing my personal key success and failure factors I can easily tell when I am following my LightPath and when I am following my DarkPath. I am extremely fortunate to know my purpose and to be able to live it fully and with love.

Darlene, compassionate caretaker and inspirational manager

As we grow and evolve and work through our SolePath key factors, they change. We have found that identifying these key factors, once a year, highlights our progress and personal growth as we work through our DarkPath and renews our focus for living in our LightPaths.

SolePath community

Another focus of our SolePath work has been creating community. We have discovered, as more and more have begun their SolePath journey, that one of our deepest needs is a sense of belonging, a need for others to know who we are, a need to have our gifts and greatness recognized, a need to reach out to others.

We have a powerful longing to connect with like-minded people, to those who understand our desire to live in expanded energy and our urge to make a difference in the world. Belonging is essential to living our beautiful life and we are connected at a deep level by our desire to be on purpose; to make a difference.

SolePath communities are being created in person and online, with the intention of encouraging each other to live beautiful lives; to support each other as we discover our purpose. SolePath communities are for those who are choosing to create their meaningful life. SolePath communities are for those who are choosing to live their life at a higher vibration. SolePath communities gather together, reach out to each other and provide a place of belonging, of not feeling alone as we walk our path to purpose.

It is a truth that we live and experience our SolePath through our interaction with others. Fundamentally, we are who we are because of our connection to others. Our SolePath is who we are born to be. Our purpose is revealed in our interaction with others.

YOU ARE LOVED. IT IS THE HUMAN EXPERIENCE TO FORGET THIS. IT IS OFTEN IN RITUAL THAT A REMEMBERING OF THE LOVE OF GOD OCCURS. THIS IS IMPORTANT. AS YOU HAVE GROWN AWAY FROM TRADITIONS, AWAY FROM COMMUNITY, TOWARDS SELF, YOU HAVE LOST THIS. MEANINGFUL ACTIONS ARE WHAT BECOME MEANINGFUL RITUAL. IT IS A NEED AND THERE IS A YEARNING FOR THIS; RITUAL AND CEREMONY BECOME SACRED BEHAVIOURS.

RITUAL IS LACKING FOR THOSE WHO NO LONGER FEEL WELCOME WITHIN THE RITUAL OF RELIGION. IT IS NEEDED. THE RHYTHM OF A PARTICULAR DAY FOR REST, THE RHYTHM OF A PARTICULAR PLACE THAT PROVIDES SANCTUARY; A GATHERING TOGETHER WITH A COMMON PURPOSE.

MAKE TIME FOR FUN; FOR HAVING FUN TOGETHER. CEREMONY AND RITUAL HAVE THESE PURPOSES: RHYTHM, SANCTUARY, CONNECTION WITH EACH OTHER AND WITH US. COULD THIS NOT ALSO BE FUN?

SET INTENTION FOR GATHERING TOGETHER IN COMMUNITY, FOR SIMPLY CONNECTING WITH OTHER SOULS ON THE SAME JOURNEY.

SETH

SolePath communities create activities and topics that stimulate conversation around living with purpose. They have rhythm – regular behaviour and habits that can be counted on; they provide sanctuary – a sense of belonging;

they provide connection — to each other and to 'what you cannot see'.

The SolePath community code for participants is to be present in expanding energy, participate in my LightPaths, to be my best. To participate, fully determined to be 'all in'. To show respect to all present, to treat others as I would like to be treated. To walk the talk, to always ensure that my words and actions are a match. To leave all distractions at the door.

The SolePath community pledge is to honour the gifts and greatness of all present. To see all in the gathering as perfect eternal souls having an earth experience and doing the best that they can. To honour the shared purpose and intention of the gathering. Because who knows what we can accomplish together, for us all.

As you manifest your great truth, think about creating community. Not only for those you are assisting with your wisdom, but also for yourself. It can sometimes be lonely.

SolePath daily ritual

During the focus one to nine mentoring process, we share many practical tools for integrating SolePath into everyday life; for applying the theoretical SolePath learning and putting it into action.

As your great truth evolves, provide practical help. Share the tools that work for you; the ones that you have tested and tried. We need practical things that we can do; daily ritual and ceremony to help us understand ourselves better and feel happier.

Here is an example of an easy, quick, effective morning ritual. This focuses on expanding energy, the LightPaths, and sets the energetic tone for the day.

In ancient cultures, the word for god was the same as 'I Am'. Begin your day by stating your SolePath 'I Am' statement, followed by the question 'how may I serve?'

As an example, here is mine: I am an inspirational teacher and a spiritual mystic; how may I serve?. John's is: I am a charismatic adventurer and intellectual lateral thinker; how may I serve?

Next, complete this quick thankfulness meditation.

Sit quietly, with both feet on the ground and your hands resting gently in your lap. Close your eyes softly with your eyelids relaxed. Relax your jaw, soften your lips and feel your scalp relaxing.

Notice the breath going in and out of your body, cooler as it goes in, warmer as it comes out. Imagine that you are breathing in bright white light that it is filling up your body. Imagine that you are breathing out dark energy that you no longer need.

If you have a charismatic SolePath, adventurer, gladiator, influencer, leader or performer, imagine that you are inside a shell, like the shell of an egg, and place your focus on this safe, exterior covering. Express thankfulness for who you are, for your charismatic self and the life you are living.

If you have a compassionate SolePath, caretaker, facilitator or healer, place your hand and your focus on your heart. Express thankfulness for who you are, for your loving self and the life you are living.

If you have an inspirational SolePath, conformist, humanitarian, manager or teacher, place your hands and your focus on your adrenal glands (middle of your back on either side of your spine). Straighten your spine and express thankfulness for who you are, for your inspiring self and the life you are living.

If you have an intellectual SolePath, controller, expert or lateral thinker, place your focus on your pineal gland (shaped like a tiny pine cone, between the two hemispheres near the centre of your brain). Express thankfulness for who you are, for your great mind and the life you are living.

If you have an intuitive SolePath, creator, builder, hunter or solitude, place your hand and your focus on your solar plexus. Express thankfulness for who you are, for your wise intuitive self and the life you are living.

If you have a spiritual SolePath, balance, mystic or warrior, place your focus and your finger on your third eye (the space between your eyebrows). Express thankfulness for who you are, for your connected self and the life you are living.

As Seth would say, you are safe and all is well.

Some of us have two LightPaths from different categories, just like John and I. Some of us have double LightPaths, just like our certified analysts who have double spiritual SolePaths. When doing your morning ritual, if you have two different categories, simply alternate your body focus, or choose the focus that feels best in the moment, or do them both together.

The body focus is a physical point on our body that connects us directly to our soul, our wisdom. It is different for each of us depending on our SolePath categories.

Dr. Debra Ford Msc.D

One of my clients is a traditional chinese medicine doctor and one of her LightPaths is inspirational conformist. She is building on what other traditional chinese medicine doctors have done before, expanding the body of work as she creates healing for her patients.

She came for her mentoring session and we talked about inspirationals being the role models of society, of how these category SolePaths are the figurative bones of our society, providing structure and order.

We ended our session by completing her thankfulness meditation together, she obediently placed her hands in the middle of her back and put her focus on her adrenals situated above her kidneys. She closed her eyes and instead of settling in to her meditation, she asked 'Did you know that in chinese medicine the kidneys assist with bone strength?'

No, I didn't, I only know that inspirational SolePaths are the bones of society and that this is the place on their body that connects them directly to their soul.

What SolePath has meant for others

Ask others how your truth has helped. Sometimes breaking new ground can be lonely work and it is a great reminder to hear from others how you have made a difference in their lives. At the time of writing, we have completed just over 1,000 SolePaths. For many, SolePath has been the missing piece in their life's journey; SolePath is their truth; but SolePath is not for everyone.

Teachings that have been passed down over the centuries bring forward the beautiful energy of all who have participated in them. And this is a beautiful experience. It is very important to remember that there is no one truth.

Truth is only your truth — in the moment, at this time in your life, here and now. And your truth is based on everything that brings you to the now.

There is no need to let go of all that has gone before, but rather to build on what has gone before. Every new truth begins from building on what has gone before. As you move forward in your life, what has gone before is always fundamental to the purposeful moving forward. A truth will emerge for you that is the perfect merging of all past and future experiences.

SETH

Your teaching, your great truth, will not be for everyone. Allow that to be so; find a way to be okay with that; focus on those who need your wisdom. All is well.

I would like to extend my gratitude to you both for the gift of SolePath. I am currently working with one of your SolePath certified mentors on my SolePath journey. My experience thus far has brought forth clarity, stability and a trust that is guiding me back on my path into expansive light. I feel a sweet lifting and greater understanding of my connection to Self and Source through the work I have been able to do and look forward to the steadiness and expansion that is unfolding. I am blessed to be in this space of learning and receptivity of the power of SolePath. With deep thanks.

Kristen, intuitive creator and inspirational teacher

Dr. Debra Ford Msc.D

There have been some big shifts in my life that have made me much more happy and feeling balanced in life. And, I attribute those shifts directly to the last coaching session we had! I have not only changed jobs but have shifted entire careers. The last time we spoke you encouraged me to think about what else an inspirational manager and compassionate healer could contribute to for work ... and the first thing that came to mind was marketing. Without me looking for it, a position came to me – and I am now the Marketing and Development Specialist at a non-profit that provides health and social services to low-income, homeless and uninsured. It feels amazing to work for an organization that makes such a positive difference in the community. (!) With appreciation!

Liz, inspirational manager and compassionate healer

Since I discovered my SolePath, I have had such a different direction in life. I have much more confidence in knowing that I am who I am, and that is enough! It is an amazing feeling and I would love to share that with others.

Ashley, spiritual balance and intellectual expert

The teachings of SolePath provided me with both confirmation and permission to pursue a path of value and meaning. I now have an internal compass that enables me to choose in the direction of my light and not only feel incredibly joyful, but also of service. The teaching has come at such a crucial time, when we can no longer afford to search for our light. We need to live it.

Tanis, spiritual balance and spiritual mystic

SolePath has been very helpful in understanding what makes me joyful. I can now listen to my intuition and hear when I need to take a break from my everyday duties and do something that speaks to me in my life, to ensure it fits my soul's path.

Brady, intuitive creator and spiritual mystic

Thank you so much for your (SolePath energy) analysis! I must admit it took me a few days to see the light since your analysis of my LightPaths was so far off from how I perceived myself. But then it hit me — that's why I am unhappy and not content with my life (work and social) and that I have to rethink myself and follow my LightPaths. Funny though, the DarkPath I could relate to right away! Thank you so much. Now I have to be brave and make the changes!

Antje, inspirational humanitarian and compassionate healer

SolePath builds healthy communication in relationships. It provides a new and interesting context in which you can understand and relate to your partner in exciting ways. I found my SolePath energy analysis for me and my partner to be as useful as couples counseling, for the fresh view point it offers not only of yourself, but also of the one you love!

Curran, charismatic gladiator and intellectual lateral thinker; Lisa, his partner, compassionate facilitator and inspirational teacher

Dr. Debra Ford Msc.D

I was caught off guard at that moment of emotion. Some truths run deep. The awareness of moving toward beauty and possibility has been a beacon through the dark and has so much strength and light for me. It's like a flashing sign saying 'go that way'. What you have shared is a gift. With each continued experience the fullness of the work you are doing takes my breath away. Striving to live purposefully.

Celeste, intuitive builder and intuitive creator

Dr. Debra Ford Msc.D

SECTION 5 – SOLEPATH AND LIFE

- Healing
- Counseling
- Education
- Business and human resources
- Yoga
- Addiction and recovery
- Athletes and sports teams
- Animal behaviour
- Travel

NAVIGATION: IT IS THE KNOWLEDGE, IT IS THE BOUNDARY
WITHIN WHICH YOU WILL FLOW, IT IS THE WAY AHEAD.
SOLEPATH IS THE PATH.
SETH

Dr. Debra Ford Msc.D

SECTION 5 – SOLEPATH AND LIFE

As SolePath has grown and expanded, I have become really conscientious at simply writing the inspiration down; not always having to know where each piece fits into the work; being patient and seeing where it leads. Yes! Following the next breadcrumb.

As your great truth manifests, get really good at keeping notes, let it unfold, take the next step. Write something and set is aside until you know where it fits in; allow the inspiration to flow. In writing this book I used some notes from two years ago, not having any idea why I was writing them back then. I am smiling as I write this, because I know how hard this might be for our intellectuals, those of you who are our great minds, our logical and linear thinkers. Breathe.

As the SolePath body of work has expanded, as more people have been attracted to SolePath, including healers, councilors, educators, business consultants, animal workers, new applications for SolePath have been created.

SolePath is not a belief system, it is a navigation tool, so it can be applied in all situations, it can simply be layered right on top of other amazing truths.

Healing

As Seth has taught us, our place of energetic collapse, our DarkPath is where we are vulnerable to mental and physical ill health. We are finding a predisposition to certain types of illnesses depending on the SolePath category. The list below is for information and must be managed under the care of a trusted health care professional.

DarkPath health vulnerabilities

Charismatic category dis-ease

Mental health predisposition	Physical health vulnerability
Attention deficit disorder	Skin disorders including eczema, acne
Addictions	Liver disease
Exhibitionism including hyperactivity	Gallbladder
Unstable behaviour	Pancreas including diabetes
Stuttering	Spleen

Compassionate category dis-ease

Mental health predisposition	Physical health vulnerability
Fear	Heart disease
Sexual obsessions	Blood disorders including anemia, cholesterol, hemophilia, bruising, nose bleeds
Antisocial behaviour	Female issues including breasts, reproductive system, infertility
Immaturity, dependence on family	Male issues including prostate, impotence
Over sensitivity	Fainting

Inspirational category dis-ease

Mental health predisposition	Physical health vulnerability
Anger	Structural or bone disorders including osteoporosis
Suspicion, secrecy	Joint disorders including arthritis, gout
Loss of contact with reality	Back pain
Fear of change	Kidneys, bladder, adrenals
Exhaustion	Premature greying

Dr. Debra Ford Msc.D

Intellectual category dis-ease

Mental health predisposition	Physical health vulnerability
Sleep disorders including insomnia	Headaches including migraine and cluster
Eating disorders including anorexia	Multiple sclerosis
Inferiority or superiority complex	Alzheimer's
Obsessive control, jealousy	Stroke
Tendency to harm	Lou Gehrig's disease

Intuitive category dis-ease

Mental health predisposition	Physical health vulnerability
Moodiness and irritability	Digestive disorders including heartburn, constipation, ulcers, diarrhea, colitis
Depression	Food intolerances and allergies
Laziness	Crohns disease
Suicidal tendencies	Glandular disorders including mononucleosis, lymphatic disease, thyroid
Panic attacks	Excessive sweating

Spiritual category dis-ease

Mental health predisposition	Physical health vulnerability
Fear of death and illness	Breathing and lung disorders including asthma, coughs
Lack of integrity	Colds and flu
Dogma and radical fundamentalism	Ear disorders including hearing loss
Nightmares	Eye disorders including cataracts and vision loss
Inability to cope with life	Mouth disorders including jaw and teeth

Our SolePath certified mentors work hand in hand with holistic healers to assist with healing by providing guidance on how to reach for LightPaths, a place of energetic expansion; the energetic place where body and mind can heal.

Ultimately with the right combination of health care providers and living life in expanded energy, in the LightPaths, great mental and physical health can be for everyone.

How do you know if someone is living in their LightPaths or DarkPath? Just ask the question 'how healthy are they?' Even for yourself, when you get a headache or pain in your shoulder, ask 'why am I responding to this from my DarkPath?' Then choose something else.

YOU CAN'T UNDERSTAND ILLNESS UNTIL YOU KNOW WHAT CAUSES ENERGY TO COLLAPSE; YOU WON'T KNOW HOW TO HEAL UNTIL YOU KNOW WHAT YOUR DARKPATH IS.

SETH

Counseling

When SolePath was created we had no idea how helpful it would be in building better relationships. SolePath is certainly all about the individual person and who they were born to be; it is a personal analysis that provides understanding about individual behaviour but it also gives deep insights into relationships; into understandings about interaction and behavior.

In relationships, SolePath provides keys to communication and understanding.

Dr. Debra Ford Msc.D

SolePath for successful relationships

Romantic relationships

In romance, SolePath is a fundamental tool for forming successful, lasting and fulfilling relationships; it provides the navigation for a peaceful, loving and joyful relationship. It is a stunning truth that we usually fall in love with someone because they are different from us and this makes them interesting; then we spend most of our relationship together trying to make them be just like us. To think like us, to like what we like ...

SolePath provides a critical link for understanding behaviour that leads to relationship success. When each of us knows what makes us joyful and then understands what makes our partner joyful, the chance of a successful relationship is so much greater.

SolePath also crosses the artificial barriers we have created between genders, where men have to be strong and women have to be taken care of. SolePath allows us to be who we are in our most intimate relationships.

Parenting

In parenting, we believe that our only responsibility to our children is to love them and keep them physically safe. Our children are wise and each generation seems to be born with more insights than the one before.

THEY (YOUR CHILDREN) ARE (WISE) AND THEY WILL MANIFEST THIS IN THEIR LIVES, THIS KNOWING IS DEEPLY IMPRINTED FOR THEM. THEY ARE BUILDING ON THE LIGHT ALREADY GROWING ON EARTH, THEY ARE GLOWING ALREADY; ALL IS IN PLACE; ALL IS WELL.

YOUR YOUTH ARE MORE THAN OKAY, THEY ARE FACILITATING THE

CHANGE THAT WE DESIRE. WITH THEIR OPENNESS, OPEN MINDS, OPEN HEARTS, AND THEIR REJECTION OF THE VALUES THAT THEIR PARENTS HOLD. THESE YOUNGER AGE SOULS, YOUNG IN EARTH YEARS, WILL BE A CATALYST FOR EVOLUTION. EVOLUTION OF THE ALL, THE UNIVERSE.

THEY DO NOT RESIST. THEY DO NOT LIVE IN FEAR OF CHANGE. THEY ARE EXPERIENTIAL. YOU ARE ALL ON EARTH FOR INDIVIDUAL EXPERIENCE AND FOR COLLECTIVE EXPERIENCE AND THE COLLECTIVE EXPERIENCE SHIFTS DEPENDING ON WHAT HAS GONE BEFORE. NOW, LIGHT IS NEEDED ON YOUR PLANET. ALL SOULS KNOW THIS. YOUR YOUNG KNOW HOW TO DO THIS.

SETH

Our responsibility as parents is to allow our children to be who they were born to be.

EXPECTATION COMES FROM MANY SOURCES; EXPECTATION OF PARENTS, EMPLOYERS, PARTNERS, GOVERNMENTS. IT IS MORE A FACT OF WHAT THE WORLD AND OTHERS EXPECT FROM YOU. PARENTS HAVE EXPECTATIONS OF CHILDREN RATHER THAN ALLOWING THE CHILD TO USE THEIR GIFTS AND GREATNESS. THERE IS SO MUCH EXPECTATION AND IN THAT, THERE IS SO MUCH BURDEN PLACED ON SELF.

SETH

It is possible that prior to seven or eight years of age, children are more connected to their LightPaths than their DarkPath. However as the conscious mind kicks in and the expectations of the outside world become more demanding, the sub-conscious DarkPath begins to have a bigger impact on behaviour. Of course, this depends on the child's environment and whether they are allowed to be who they are born to be.

Children being born now are more evolved and less likely to be stuck in old patterns.

Dr. Debra Ford Msc.D

As we talk with parents, we have wondered about when a soul enters the body during pregnancy and what affect this might have on parenting children. Here is what we understand at this time.

There are some souls that enter the body at conception. These souls are connected to and identify with their body. They participate in the birth process and want to experience all of it, including the shock of being born.

When they are born these souls have more control over their body, are settled within their body and keen to participate in physical existence. They are emotional, impatient and practical souls. These children are likely to have an intuitive, intellectual, inspirational or charismatic SolePath.

There are other souls who wait to enter the body. These souls are disconnected and independent of their body. They are observers of the birth process and act in a supportive role, connected to but separate from their physical body.

These souls are slower to obtain control over their body and identify with their body and physical existence. They are dreamers, philosophers and live in a fantasy world; they are sometimes eccentric, often different and mostly reserved. These children are likely to have a spiritual or compassionate SolePath.

Of course, there are souls which enter their body at other times during the pregnancy, whenever they feel ready.

Understanding this process of integration by a soul into the body could have a significant impact on how and when each individual learns basic physical survival skills. This understanding may help parents cope with some of the key crisis points and expectations might be avoided, such as at what age they will potty train, when they will start to walk and talk, why some children don't like to sleep alone or are more prone to night terrors.

Family relationships

Some families have intertwined SolePaths and some have no SolePath connection at all and the reasons for this are obscure. Some families share categories and some share actual SolePaths. For some family members the path could manifest as a LightPath and for others it could manifest as a DarkPath.

In whatever way the SolePaths interact, knowing who each family member was born to be provides the foundation for healthy, loving family relationships. When I know who you are and you know who I am, our only responsibility is to create a family in which we can each live in our own different greatness.

As an example, this is our family chart:

Debra	Inspirational teacher and spiritual mystic	Dark compassionate healer
John	Charismatic adventurer and intellectual lateral thinker	Dark intellectual controller
Joel	Compassionate facilitator and intuitive builder	Dark charismatic gladiator
Adam	Intuitive hunter and charismatic leader	Dark inspirational humanitarian

Dr. Debra Ford Msc.D

Just a few observations about our family ...

Both Joel and Adam have intuitive LightPaths. As parents we need to allow them to trust their intuition with regard to people, experiences and opportunities, rather than impose our own observations and values on them.

As a compassionate facilitator, Joel's family always comes first. As a dark inspirational humanitarian, Adam's family always comes last. By focusing on his LightPath, Adam has made his family an integral part of his intuitive hunter's community.

As a charismatic leader, Adam is a bright flame who is fun to be around. As a dark charismatic gladiator, Joel can turn off his light no matter how his darkness affects those around him. By focusing on his LightPath, Joel's compassionate facilitator makes a happy community a top priority.

John has an intellectual SolePath in his LightPath and DarkPath and he is a member of mensa, an exclusive intellectual society. One of the characteristics of being a dark intellectual is a natural predisposition towards being critical. This is important for him to be aware of when dealing with our sons who are successful adults who don't necessarily think the same way that he does. Our sons are constantly picking John's brain for his innovative ideas and considerable business experience.

As for me, a dark compassionate healer, it is possible to smother those I love and that's all I am going to say about that! I am certain that I am going to be a wonderful grandmother.

Parents need to love their children and to keep them physically safe; also to allow them and encourage them to be fully in their LightPaths greatness. It is very unlikely that children will think, feel or react to the world in the same way that their parents do. They may even have very different values; and that's okay; actually it isn't just okay; it's perfect. If only all parents understood that.

Our family does not have too many SolePath connections but some families like the one below shows just how entangled family SolePaths can be.

Mom	Inspirational humanitarian and spiritual balance	Dark intuitive solitude
Dad	Inspirational teacher and spiritual warrior	Dark charismatic influencer
Child	Inspirational humanitarian and spiritual warrior	Dark inspirational teacher
Child	Inspirational humanitarian and inspirational conformist	Dark spiritual balance

This family would certainly find it easy to enjoy each other's company in their LightPaths and share a common goal. They all need a cause to work on and they can do it together. Both the inspirational humanitarian and spiritual warrior are living with purpose when working on a cause for the greater good.

On the other hand, their DarkPaths are all so entirely different and this knowledge provides a great focus for family counseling.

SolePath Ancestry

Councilors are familiar with the genetic predisposition to both mental and physical illnesses that run in families, but

Dr. Debra Ford Msc.D

what about the SolePath threads that connect family members? Not only the SolePath predisposition to illness, but also to gifts and greatness.

There is a great deal of interest in ancestory and SolePath could add a very interesting dimension and insight into the fame and fortunes of families.

Looking further than immediate family, examining what ancestors accomplished in their lives, living in their LightPaths or their DarkPath, could provide many clues to mental and emotional health.

With a photograph, we can measure the SolePath of ancestors, but we have been advised by Seth not to complete the SolePath energy analysis for anyone who has been deceased more than two hundred years.

Seth tells us that most of us are reincarnating every two to three hundred years and SolePath is part of an earth life's plan. It may be that we would receive an incorrect reading, as it could be the SolePath of the deceased ancestor, or the new path that the soul is living in their next incarnation.

Education

I know that if you are an educator, you dream of a learning environment in which all are celebrated for their own unique gifts and greatness; a learning environment where all are able to absorb through their own unique path and learning style. We can help. Each SolePath category has a distinct learning style.

SolePath learning styles

Charismatics need to review, reflect, observe and are visual learners. They need an environment that allows them to shine, but they also require the boundaries that help them to not overpower others in the group. They love ideas and interesting, engaging content with lots of variety, particularly if it is relevant to themselves and their own life experience.

Compassionates need to learn in a people oriented environment with plenty of opportunities for networking and participating. They are kinesthetic learners and need to feel comfortable in a nurturing classroom environment. They love opportunities to create relationships, in their own time, and are most engaged when the subject of the learning is people centred.

Inspirationals are practical doers who need to finish tasks; they are accomplishers who are visual learners. They need an organized classroom environment where they know what is expected of them. They love knowing what they are going to learn, what the goals are for the classroom and the purpose of the teachings. They thrive in a structured environment with content and agenda.

Intellectuals love anything that stimulates intellect; they are the pure theoretical learners, although they do prefer topics that are relevant to their interests. They are logical thinkers and auditory learners who need a quiet environment with limited distractions. They need to be acknowledged for their intellect and to feel heard. Intellectuals love to debate and discuss both sides of a situation, just for the joy of it.

Intuitives are experiential kinesthetic learners who need to explore ideas. They are hands-on learners who like to see their ideas manifest and become practically real. They need to feel safe and require encouragement and positive reinforcement for their contribution. They love engaging and open-ended content with the opportunity to explore and share their own ideas.

Spirituals are conceptual, impressionistic, auditory learners who thrive in an abstract and somewhat unstructured environment. They love to listen, but need to be encouraged to participate with others in the classroom or they will remain in their own little world. A wide range of content and exposure to multiple ideas and concepts will keep Spirituals engaged.

Anecdotally, what we are seeing in the mentoring process is that adults with intellectual SolePaths sometimes have difficulty acknowledging that they are one of the world's great minds. Often, they did not thrive at school; they were bored and did just enough to obtain a passing grade. Sometimes they flew through school without being engaged or making any effort. They also may have dropped out long before graduation and feel that they are stupid as a result. How disturbing that our great minds are not being served by most learning environments, and what incredible potential if we could just tap into this intellectual greatness.

As the energy on our planet moves from I to we; from a focus on me to a focus on all of us; bringing out the gifts and greatness as we educate our children could be the most significant thing we do to really facilitate this societal change.

Business and human resources

We understand that everything is energy, that energy is common to all things and this allows us to measure the SolePath of a business and the business culture.

SolePath for business strategy

Every business has a culture. Every business has a SolePath. Every business has a specific energy vibration that guides the business to greatness. The SolePath of a business uncovers the key business strengths and helps define the business purpose and identifies opportunities for success.

The SolePath of a business provides direction for goals, strategy and implementation. Our business, SolePath, is an inspirational teacher and spiritual mystic, dark inspirational manager. Our strategy is guided by our understanding that we need to stay focused on communicating this sacred body of work and to ask for help with getting SolePath out into the world.

The SolePath institute is a spiritual mystic and spiritual balance, dark intuitive hunter. The business strategy here is to be a spiritual organization; to simply be unapologetically metaphysical; and to allow the institute to flow in natural energy cycles. Attention to detail will always be critical.

This book, SolePath - the path to purpose and a beautiful life, is a triple spiritual; a spiritual mystic and spiritual warrior, dark spiritual balance. The intention for this book is to motivate others to manifest their spiritual work; for us to stand up for our cause, SolePath, and to be an assertive and strong decision maker.

Our SolePath facebook community is an inspirational teacher and spiritual mystic, dark intellectual controller. Our strategy on facebook is to share our teachings and spiritual wisdom through this forum, to engage in SolePath conversations and not to define and control this community too closely. Very difficult for John's dark intellectual controller.

The SolePath community group that meets in Red Deer,

Dr. Debra Ford Msc.D

Alberta, Canada is an inspirational teacher and spiritual mystic, dark intuitive solitude. Our strategy for this community group is to communicate our spiritual teachings and to engage all spiritual seekers, to connect with everyone who wants to live their life at a higher vibration, not just those who have had their SolePath energy analysis completed.

SolePantry is a compassionate healer and intuitive builder, dark intuitive solitude. The strategy for the SolePantry, a company that provides all of the practical tools for living in a place of expanded energy, is to focus on tools for mental, physical and metaphysical healing and to allow possibilities to emerge; to stay connected to the SolePath institute and not to operate separately and alone.

Your great truth will also have its own SolePath that will be a wonderful guide for your success strategy.

SolePath for business relationships

Another way that SolePath helps in the business environment is with business relationships. It is a guide for bringing out the best in an employee, to help them work in their LightPaths and avoid their very familiar, collapsing DarkPath skills.

Because our DarkPath is a mastered skill that is easy to do, it plays a huge role in our career choice. We do the personality tests at school, show these incredible skills, choose that university degree and then end up in occupations fairly and squarely in our DarkPaths, jobs that we just don't enjoy and can't even imagine why that might be. Something just isn't right.

A board of directors we worked with a few years ago had a financial controller who was a dark intellectual expert and a human resources director who was a dark compassionate caretaker. It was work that they were good at, the DarkPath is a familiar place of skill, but both of these women hated their jobs and were counting down the days till retirement.

For the employer, SolePath highlights the fundamental keys to identifying the right person for the right job. This results in job satisfaction for the candidate and company satisfaction with the employee who will stay engaged in their work and loyal to the company.

As in personal relationships, SolePath also assists with inter company communication; how to speak to each individual in a way that they can hear.

Yoga

Yoga provides a way to unite you with your soul using mental, physical and spiritual practice. SolePath is living your life to have the experience your soul intended.

Yoga is the path to inner peace and a perfect tool for placing you in the present moment, the now. And it is only from the moment of now that you can choose your LightPaths and contribute to the change of energy on our planet. SolePath provides clarity, a direction, a focus, an affirming of who you are born to be, of your true being.

Yoga is now, me; SolePath is direction, us. When SolePath and yoga are combined it facilitates your inner light; allowing the soul to speak so that you can fulfill your life's purpose of sharing your gifts and greatness.

The true benefit of practicing yoga and knowing your SolePath is that life can be lived, not only on the mat, but

Dr. Debra Ford Msc.D

also to the fullest from your LightPaths everyday. Yoga is a way of life; SolePath is the direction for your lifetime. Yoga provides a way to cast off your daily struggles and SolePath bring awareness of your true divine self.

SolePath not only provides direction for individual yoga practice but is also an amazing tool for yoga teacher training. It guides each student to know their gifts and greatness and to become a better teacher; it provides a perspective from which to teach. A class taught by a charismatic is going to be very different from that of a compassionate, and what wonderful variety to offer students.

I SAY YOU MUST LIVE DIFFERENTLY. I AM ASKING ALL OF THESE LIGHT WORKERS TO LIVE DIFFERENTLY. YOUR PLANET IS DEPENDING ON YOU ALL DOING THIS DIFFERENTLY. IT IS POSSIBLE. NOW IS THE TIME.

SETH

Addiction and recovery

Addiction is generally defined as the continued use of a substance or engaging in a behaviour, despite the adverse consequences for the individual or those around them. Addictions include drugs and alcohol, food, sex, gambling or any compulsive behaviours that interfere with normal life.

The charismatic SolePaths are the paths that are most likely to have physical addiction tendencies, in particular the charismatic adventurer. Other SolePath categories can also exhibit addictive tendencies but usually for emotional or psychological reasons.

Much more work and research is needed on the subject of

SolePath for addiction and recovery, and here are some anecdotes that may be helpful.

A dark intellectual controller used drugs and alcohol to control her husband's behaviour. When she was using the substances she found that her workaholic husband paid her more attention. She was using the drugs and alcohol to control him and get his attention. After counseling and with a better understanding of why she was drinking and taking drugs she was able to choose her LightPaths and different behaviour.

A dark inspirational humanitarian sat in the basement drinking dozens of beers each evening, ignoring his wife and four children upstairs. The motivation for his drinking, his dark inspirational humanitarian, was his tendency to neglect those closest to him, his family. With the understanding of why he was drinking and isolating himself from his family, he was also able to choose his LightPaths.

A light charismatic Adventurer discovered over the course of his lifetime that he had a physical addiction to food. Charismatic adventurers struggle with moderation and in all cases it is safer for them to give up the substance rather than to try to cut down, whether it be chocolate, coffee, wine, sugar or something different.

Knowing whether an addiction is physical or emotional/psychological can assist with the recovery process. Knowing the SolePath of the individual will not only help with this diagnosis but will also provide clear direction for creating a future meaningful and beautiful life after recovery. SolePath can help.

Athletes and sports teams

Both of my sons were involved in competitive team sports during their teen years, up to university level. As parents we watched as some coaches were able to motivate them to excellence, while others simply undermined their confidence.

Most coaches use a consistent and standard approach for all of the athletes under their care, some of the individuals thrive, some of them collapse, and it doesn't usually have anything to do with athletic ability.

Knowing the SolePath of an athlete provides incredible insights into motivating them. For our eldest son, a compassionate facilitator, he would have moved mountains for the other players on the team as his life's primary motivation is creating and contributing to his community.

Joel is also a dark charismatic gladiator, who is choosing away from his ruthless desire to win. So a focus on winning may have been a great way to push him to perform, but ultimately he had to give up his athletic dreams due to repeated sports injuries.

For our youngest son, a charismatic leader, he needed to be leading his team mates to excellence, to be leading from the front. Adam was a gifted athlete and one of the few to play on two competitive teams at university, both football and basketball. His dark inspirational humanitarian was a workaholic, prone to over training, and his challenge was navigating that delicate balance between leading the team and depleting himself. Ultimately he also injured himself and ended his athletic career.

Knowing the SolePath of an athlete not only guides as to how to motivate them but also provides clues as to their physical and mental training needs. When athletes are competing from their LightPaths they have an energetic shield that helps them maintain physical and mental health. When they engage from their DarkPath, their place of energetic collapse, they are vulnerable to injury.

As we have learned, each SolePath has a learning style that will guide the coaching and physical training. There are linguistic cues that can be used to enable vastly improved coach and athlete communication.

Talk about a competitive advantage; happy athletes, happy coaches, great outcomes.

Animal behaviour

SolePath for pets — dogs, cats, horses

For people, SolePath is who we were born to be. It is our guide to a beautiful life, filled with happiness, peace, joy, love, purpose, meaning. For pets, SolePath is a little different. It is how they interact with people in an individual, predetermined and predictable way.

Knowing a pet's SolePath is a wonderful way to understand the most joyful way in which people and animals can live, love and play together. Knowing a pet's SolePath enables a joyful interaction for the animal and the caregiver. The pet's life is made as joyful as possible and in return they are able to make the lives of the people they live with joyful too.

Pets are our companions and the collaboration between the animal energy and the human energy is the perfect example of how we can shift our focus from me to us. They teach us how to care for and love another being, and in return love us unconditionally.

Dr. Debra Ford Msc.D

Pets come to earth with a spiritual connection and they maintain this connection when they are in loving, caring human relationships. They show us how to live with balance and flow, they teach us mystical connection, they live with integrity and dedication.

Every pet is spiritual and has a connection to the field of energy. In our everyday, busy lives when we are in our DarkPath we lose our connection to source energy and pets can help us shift into our LightPaths and reconnect us to this wisdom. They fulfill many roles in our lives – particularly spiritual guide.

Dogs, cats and horses have three paths, all of which are expanding; they do not have a DarkPath. Their paths are charismatic, compassionate, inspirational, intellectual, intuitive or spiritual. For all dogs, cats and horses one of their expanding paths is the spiritual path.

Dogs have a spiritual path entwined with two other SolePath categories. For example, our dog Buddy was a spiritual, charismatic, intuitive.

Cats have a spiritual path and an inspirational path, entwined with one other of the SolePath categories. Our son's cat Mimi is a spiritual, inspirational, compassionate.

Horses have a spiritual path and an intellectual path, entwined with one other of the SolePath categories. Shriner, a horse on a working ranch for disadvantaged girls, is a spiritual, intellectual, intuitive.

A pet's SolePath is analyzed in the same way as a person, using a photograph and completed with the same care by our SolePath certified energy analysts, at the SolePath institute.

Pet communication

Remember all dogs, cats and horses have a spiritual path and because of their spiritual connection, they can and do love to 'talk' with their caregiver. Begin a conversation with them about their SolePath. Tell your pet that you know their SolePath and ask for inspiration on how you can make their life more joyful. Let them know how they can best make your life more joyful by sharing your SolePath with them. Use their SolePath and your SolePath to develop your own, private language.

Pet motivation

Add to the quality of your pet's life with healthy treats and rewards. Here are clues to their fundamental motivation.

- Charismatics exist to add sparkle and light to your life. They reflect back what is going on in your life and are a mirror for how you are feeling and behaving, whether you are interacting with them from your LightPaths or your DarkPath.

- Compassionates exist to please. They love to love and are likely to have hurt feelings if you are interacting with them from your DarkPath rather than your LightPaths.

- Inspirationals exist to serve and be useful. They will make your life a joy and delight if you encourage them to help and make them feel needed. Look in your own LightPaths for ways in which they can serve you.

- Intellectuals exist to please themselves but will please you to get what they want. They are complicated animals who are very intriguing and smart and will challenge you to be in your LightPaths.

Dr. Debra Ford Msc.D

- Intuitives exist to run, play and eat. They are physical animals that love their bodies. They encourage you to interact with them from your LightPaths and to lead a healthy lifestyle with lots of exercise and time outdoors.

Cherishing your pet

All pets love to be touched and comforted. And here is the best way to fill that need for each unique beloved animal.

- Charismatics will let you know when they need touching, stroking and caressing. Charismatic animals always reflect back what you are feeling, so if you are in the mood for a bit of cherishing, they will be too.
- Compassionates love frequent soft touching, stroking, caressing which can be initiated by you or by them. They need a physical connection and closeness to you.
- Inspirationals will want to be touched and caressed only when they want to be touched and caressed. Give them this love when they ask for it, but don't be surprised if they move away when they have had enough.
- Intellectuals love to be touched, but will control and initiate how and when that occurs. They allow touching and caressing in their own way, on their own terms.
- Intuitives enjoy robust touching, stroking and caressing. Intuitive animals love to be massaged because they depend upon their body feeling well.

Connecting with your pet

Spending quality time with your pets is essential and can be
so much fun for both them and you, their caregiver.

- Charismatics are the fun animals who love to play. If
  you are enjoying yourself, they are too.
- Compassionates love any time with you near them or
  touching them, this is perfect connecting time for
  these animals. They simply love to be with you.
- Inspirationals need to be of service. They love to be
  useful, so teaching and motivating them is their
  perfect connecting time with you. They need your
  time.
- Intellectuals must have mental stimulation and they
  love to solve puzzles and exercise their minds.
- Intuitives need hard exercise, with you along, this is
  the best connecting time for these animals. They just
  love to work their body hard and then have a rub
  down or massage afterwards.

Rest for your pet

Pets need rest, relaxation and sleep and here is the best way
to provide that support and care.

- Charismatics need a quiet place to be still and
  relaxed. As they are mirrors for you, they need to be
  removed to a quiet space to really relax and get the
  deep rest that they need.
- Compassionates need to be close to you or other
  animals to get their best rest.
- Inspirationals need a quiet place for escape, for
  getting away from the responsibility of serving others.

- Intellectuals need to be left alone, unless they actively come to you for interaction. They will respond poorly to being woken from sleep.
- Intuitives will sleep lots and often, anywhere and anytime. When they are awake they are 'busy, busy, busy'.

Feeding your pet

While organic foods are best for most pets, here are some other suggestions to make food more interesting and joyful.

- Charismatics get easily bored with the same food over and over again. Keep their diet interesting to keep them healthy and eating well.
- **Compassionates will eat what you ask them to eat; they will eat when you ask them to eat; they will feed to please you.**
- Inspirationals need familiar surroundings and people to feel comfortable when eating.
- Intellectuals will create their own routine and distinct habits around feeding. They thrive when that feeding routine is undisturbed.
- Intuitives are most affected by diet. With the help of a professional, choose their healthy nutrition carefully.

Pet routine

As a general rule, pets love routine because it lets them know what to expect and what to look forward to. Within a consistent time to eat and exercise, here are some suggestions.

- Charismatics are easily bored when everything stays the same. Allow them to experience new and interesting environments, walks, people, places, games and toys.
- Compassionates are content when they are with their loved ones, so will fit in with any routine as long as they are not alone.
- Inspirationals must have structure in their lives; familiar environments, walks, people, places and routines.
- Intellectuals will establish their own routine and comfort zone. Intellectual animals are essentially creatures of habit. Pay attention to what their habits are and create a life where they can enjoy them.
- Intuitives must have a routine that includes regular feeding, vigorous exercise and plenty of rest.

Pet behaviour

Pets generally reflect back to us what is going on in our own lives and if there is unhappiness ...

- Charismatics will sense this unhappiness and act out what is going on with you.
- Compassionates will feel the unhappiness deeply themselves, will try to comfort you and will hate being left alone.
- Inspirationals will become needy, as they sense the unhappiness and are not sure how to help.
- Intellectuals will withdraw into themselves.

Dr. Debra Ford Msc.D

- Intuitives will feel unhappiness in their bodies and could manifest upset tummies, injuries or other illnesses.

This SolePath knowing is the perfect complement to the tools and techniques used by animal behaviour consultants, or for anyone working to create a better life for their own beloved pets.

Travel

For places, the SolePath energy of the land permeates and impacts the people. The SolePath of a region, country, city or town is reflected in the laws and how they are implemented; the traditions and ceremonies that are embraced; childrearing and socialization; gender relations and etiquette; language dialects and cultural diversity; social structures, customs and beliefs; economic and political organization.

Awareness of these cultural tendencies provides a navigation framework for making the best decisions when living in, travelling to or doing business in a location. There is so much more joy and prosperity in a place where the culture, politics, laws and people flow with the SolePath rather than fighting against it.

Here are the SolePaths of the countries that we have analyzed.

SolePath for Places

Argentina	Intellectual lateral thinker and compassionate caretaker	Dark inspirational manager
Australia	Charismatic leader and intellectual lateral thinker	Dark intuitive builder
Bali	Compassionate facilitator and intuitive builder	Dark spiritual mystic
Belize	Charismatic adventurer and intuitive builder	Dark inspirational humanitarian
Brazil	Charismatic gladiator and intuitive creator	Dark spiritual balance
Canada	Inspirational teacher and charismatic leader	Dark compassionate facilitator
China	Inspirational manager and intuitive hunter	Dark spiritual warrior
Czech R.	Intellectual controller and charismatic adventurer	Dark inspirational conformist
Egypt	Inspirational manager and spiritual balance	Dark charismatic gladiator
England	Intuitive builder and intuitive hunter	Dark charismatic adventurer
France	Inspirational manager and intuitive builder	Dark spiritual mystic
Greece	Charismatic adventurer and intuitive builder	Dark spiritual mystic
Hong Kong	Intuitive builder and charismatic adventurer	Dark charismatic influencer
India	Intuitive hunter and spiritual mystic	Dark intellectual controller
Israel	Spiritual warrior and inspirational conformist	Dark spiritual mystic
Mexico	Spiritual balance and inspirational manager	Dark intuitive hunter
New Zealand	Spiritual warrior and intuitive creator	Dark inspirational conformist
Norway	Inspirational teacher and intuitive creator	Dark spiritual warrior
Peru	Compassionate facilitator and spiritual balance	Dark spiritual warrior
Portugal	Intuitive builder and inspirational conformist	Dark compassionate caretaker

Dr. Debra Ford Msc.D

Russia	Intellectual expert and intellectual controller	Dark inspirational conformist
Scotland	Intuitive creator and spiritual warrior	Dark compassionate caretaker
Singapore	Intellectual controller and inspirational manager	Dark intellectual expert
South Korea	Inspirational teacher and spiritual warrior	Dark charismatic gladiator
Spain	Inspirational manager and compassionate healer	Dark intuitive creator
Sweden	Compassionate facilitator and intellectual expert	Dark inspirational conformist
Taiwan	Intuitive solitude and intuitive hunter	Dark spiritual mystic
Thailand	Intuitive solitude and spiritual balance	Dark charismatic performer
USA	Compassionate facilitator and intuitive builder	Dark spiritual mystic
Wales	Intuitive solitude and intuitive hunter	Dark inspirational humanitarian

Knowing the SolePath of a place provides many insights and, if you are so inclined, a joyful exploring of the history.

LightPaths are behaviours that make the most of the gifts and greatness of a country and have a beneficial impact on its people and the world. The DarkPath is a predisposition towards behaviour that doesn't serve its people or the world.

When travelling to a place, knowing the SolePath provides clues as to how to fully enjoy your trip. When doing business in a place, knowing the SolePath allows you to discover the key success factors and key hurdles to a profitable enterprise.

SECTION 6 – SOLEPATH ENERGY TOOLS

- Pendulum
- Charismatic category
- Compassionate category
- Inspirational category
- Intellectual category
- Intuitive category
- Spiritual category
- SolePath
- Seth
- SolePlan

Evolution ... is a cooperative process, a finely tuned and constant striving for harmony between a living thing and its world.

Lynn McTaggart, the Bond

Dr. Debra Ford Msc.D

SECTION 6 – SOLEPATH ENERGY TOOLS

When I left the teachings of the christian church behind me, I decided that I did not believe in anything spiritual and simply focused on my physical life; raising my sons, struggling to get ahead with my husband, trying not to get ill. But in 1995 when I was painted into my proverbial corner with no way out; my marriage on the rocks, our business failing, our eldest son on medication for depression, our youngest son dabbling in drugs; I found a safe spiritual haven.

Feng shui became my breadcrumb; it provided me with a non-threatening way to reconnect with my higher self and source energy, through a deep understanding of the energy of my space. At that time it was so much easier for me to focus on what was going on around me, outside of me, in my space; than to try to fix the mess that was inside me.

I read all that I could on feng shui and chose what was relevant to my life. I wrote my own book called "in the feng shui zone"; created my own version called zone feng shui; created the curriculum for the first certified feng shui course taught at a college in my city and in the process annoyed everyone in the feng shui establishment because I didn't follow the rules.

This beautiful art and science saved my life and along with studying the ancient techniques of dowsing and space clearing, it was the start, it was the first breadcrumb on my new spiritual journey. I knew that it was the beginning and I never tried to see beyond it or to try to guess where it was going to lead me. I trusted and just took this first step into understanding energy and creating my new and more joyful life.

Feng shui led me to understand that if my space is divided into nine energy zones, then my life is too. My next breadcrumb was applying the principles of this ancient truth to my personal life and I wrote my doctoral dissertation on this and published my next book "the energy of intention".

As I delved deeper into eastern philosophy I became fascinated by another teaching, the wisdom of the i ching. You can imagine my delight at discovering this nebulous, flowing teaching and once again I created my own version of how to interpret it, its connection to the tao (pronounced dow) the fundamental nature of the universe, and its application in my life.

I never really understood why I always had to change what was there, why I couldn't simply fit into more traditional schools of thought, why the way that I used these ancient teachings was always different. Now, in hindsight, I understand; I was in training for this new body of work called SolePath. I just flowed downstream, not resisting; receiving the inspiration, developing a somewhat thicker skin and loving the creation process.

All this earlier learning has led me to here; the perfect place, standing on exactly the right step, to manifest the practical tools that help you choose to live in your LightPaths. As you develop your great truth, remember that we need easy tools to help facilitate positive change in our lives; mental, physical and spiritual tools.

I have already shared some of our SolePath tools with you; such as 'I am' statements; breathing techniques; a body focus for each category that connects to higher self. During our mentoring process we introduce to our clients many more tools, including meridian energy tapping and the intention process that is explained in my book 'the energy of intention'.

I would like to share with you some beautiful SolePath energy tools specially chosen to help you live in your LightPaths. Things that you can do outside of you, to balance the energy inside of you to make it easier for you to choose your LightPaths.

Everything is energy and these tools are an energy match for your SolePath. By balancing and harmonizing the natural flow of energy for your SolePath, you make it easier to choose your LightPaths.

Sometimes the tools act as a reminder, for example when you feel the gemstone in your pocket, or smell the essential oil and sometimes these beautiful energy tools just do the work for you, creating balance and harmony in your life.

For each category there is an animal instinct that gives insights into your own SolePath behaviour. Study of the category animal provides clues to behaviour that will help you gain a deeper understanding of your own instinctual energy. We use sandstone animal carvings as visual reminders of those instincts.

There is a trigram from the tao, a basic building block of creation, that depicts original natural energy. The trigram for each category provides clues to your fundamental personal characteristics and an additional layer to your understanding of who you are. We use trigram symbols as visual reminders of those characteristics.

There is a colour that enhances SolePath energy. Every colour has a wavelength and therefore a specific energy vibration. Darker colours have a softer energy and lighter colour vibrate at a higher level. Colour can be used in a variety of ways such as clothing, jewelry and artifacts. We use coloured sand in a glass jar; and it is really inspiring to look at your jar and know that these are the colours of your soul.

There is a gemstone that is an energy match for your SolePath. Gemstones are a gift from the earth, and each has a distinct energy vibration that harmonizes with the natural flow of energy of your SolePath. Your SolePath gemstones can be worn as jewelry, placed in your pocket, or simply displayed in your space. We use tumbled gemstones and carry them in a silk pouch.

There is also an essential oil, a gift from plants, that is an energy match for your SolePath. Your SolePath essential oils can be used in a diffuser, a spritzer bottle combined with filtered water, or a few drops placed on a handkerchief in your pocket. We only use organic or therapeutic grade essential oils and when combined with pure dead sea salt, you can enjoy many long, fragrant and healing baths.

There is a place in your home and office, a feng shui zone, that balances and increases the flow of energy into your life and is directly connected to your SolePath. To discover where this is located in your space, refer to my book 'in the feng shui zone'.

Pendulum

To choose the best tools for your SolePath, on any particular day, use a pendulum. It will help you choose what colour to include for your outfit, what essential oil to use on that day and which gemstone to wear or put in your pocket. Pendulums are dowsing tools that can be used by everyone, regardless of your SolePath. Pendulums are one of the oldest, simplest and most effective dowsing tools for tuning in to communication from your higher self.

Dr. Debra Ford Msc.D

There are many choices for pendulums and the best one for you will usually be your category gemstone. Therefore if you have an intellectual SolePath, an amethyst pendulum will be best; if you have an intuitive SolePath, clear quartz will be the one for you. It is such a great way to face each day with balanced energy and it only takes about sixty seconds. When you harmonize the natural flow of energy for your SolePath, choosing your LightPaths just becomes easier.

Part of our journey has been finding tools that are an energy match for each of the SolePaths; ensuring their purity and quality. In some instances we found that these tools have been difficult for clients to find.

Working with the SolePantry, all of the practical tools that we recommend are now easily available. As you develop your great truth, make sure that the tools you are recommending are accessible and the quality that you desire.

Charismatic tools: for our sparkle SolePaths who add light to life

Animal instinct = peacock

Peacocks are showy, flashy, with a deep inner wisdom, confidence and warmth.

Trigram of the tao = fire

The trigram fire denotes change. Fire is hot, explosive, bright, clear and enlightened.

Colour = red

Red is the colour of change and moving forward and it symbolizes power, strength and courage. Red commands attention yet is a friendly and warm colour. Red is the colour of blood symbolizing life, vitality and stamina. When charismatics wear red, they are able to manage their big energy and add sparkle to the lives of others.

Gemstone = tigers eye

Tigers eye encourages you to recognize your inner resources and talents and accomplish your goals. When charismatics carry tigers eye, they feel energized, full of sparkle and they feel appreciated as they interact with the world.

Essential oil = cedarwood

Cedarwood reduces fear and enhances courage. When charismatics use cedarwood they have a better sense of their inner strength.

Feng shui zone = me, myself & I

The energy for the charismatic SolePaths is found in the me,
myself & I zone of a space. The energy of this zone is all
about me and my self discovery. It is about my personal
development and getting recognition for the things that I
do.

Enhance the energy of this zone with a personal image or
artifact.

SolePath energy tools for charismatics

Animal instinct	peacock
Trigram of the tao	fire
Colour	red
Gemstone	tigers eye
Essential oil	cedarwood
Feng shui zone	me, myself & I

Compassionate tools: for our love SolePaths who respond to the world through their heart

Animal instinct = penguin

Penguins are caring, protective, patient, and comfortable in different states of consciousness.

Trigram of the tao = water

The trigram of water denotes depth. Water is flowing, fluid, reflective and sometimes still.

Colour = black

Black is about feeling fearless and protected. Black can be whatever you need it to be — it is both powerful and inconspicuous. Black encourages independence and reflection. When compassionates wear black, they are able to comfortably and safely explore their ability to trust their heart and bring love to the world.

Gemstone = black onyx

Black onyx increases personal power and builds vitality. Black onyx assists with inner strength and increases stamina. When compassionates carry black onyx they feel self-confident, centred and focused; and are better able to trust their heart.

Essential oil = rosemary

Rosemary nurtures and promotes passion for life. When compassionates use rosemary they feel purposeful, passionate and inspired.

Dr. Debra Ford Msc.D

Feng shui zone = passion & purpose

The energy for the compassionate SolePaths is found in the passion & purpose zone of a space. The energy of this zone affects our life's purpose. It helps us find our passion and assists us as we move forward on our life's journey.

Enhance the energy of this zone with a mirror or water fountain.

SolePath energy tools for compassionates

Animal instinct	penguin
Trigram of the tao	water
Colour	black
Gemstone	black onyx
Essential oil	rosemary
Feng shui zone	passion & purpose

Inspirational tools: for our role models who have a deep desire to fill a perceived need

Animal instinct = dragon

Dragons are wise and skillful, with a commanding presence; open to new ideas and possibilities, enthusiastic and vital. Of all the SolePaths the dragon is the only mythical animal.

Trigram of the tao = thunder

The trigram of thunder denotes release. Thunder is abrupt, loud, powerful and heralds nourishment.

Colour = green

Green represents growth and is the colour of life. Green is a colour that is stable and strong, yet completely flexible at the same time. Green creates feelings of hope and contentedness and it has a soothing impact on all relationships. When inspirationals wear green, they are able to stand strong and inspire us with the way that they live their lives.

Gemstone = jade

Jade encourages harmonious relationships and helps eliminate negativity. Jade assists with the flow of energy within the body. When inspirationals carry jade, they are able to see the whole picture clearly.

Essential oil = lavender

Lavender relaxes and encourages compassion. When inspirationals use lavender they see with great inner clarity.

Dr. Debra Ford Msc.D

Feng shui zone = friends & family

The energy for the inspirational SolePaths is found in the friends & family zone of a space. The energy of this zone relates to all close relationships; those that we have with our family, with our close friends, and with our co-workers. This energy is all about creating relationships that nourish and support us.

Enhance the energy of this zone with family photos that include you.

SolePath energy tools for inspirationals

Animal instinct	dragon
Trigram of the tao	thunder
Colour	green
Gemstone	jade
Essential oil	lavender
Feng shui zone	friends & family

Intellectual tools: for our great minds who can trust their ability to think things through

Animal instinct = hawk

Hawk is instinctive, calm, freedom loving; faithful and dependable, who offers sage council and advice.

Trigram of the tao = wind

The trigram of wind denotes persistence. Wind is always moving, gentle, yet can be strong and unsettling.

Colour = purple

Purple is a regal colour that commands attention and respect. Purple represents status and material wealth, while at the same time enhancing inner wisdom. Purple stimulates the mind and brings awareness of possibilities. When intellectuals wear purple, their busy brains feel soothed and they are able to explore, trust and share their thought processes.

Gemstone = amethyst

Amethyst brings good fortune and balance. Amethyst clears the personal energy field and promotes well being and happiness. When intellectuals carry amethyst, their thought processes are clear and they feel appreciated and respected.

Essential oil = orange

Orange creates a feeling of happiness and generosity. When intellectuals use orange they think joyful and positive thoughts.

Dr. Debra Ford Msc.D

Feng shui zone = wealth & happiness

The energy for the intellectual SolePaths is found in the wealth & happiness zone of a space. The energy of this zone affects all the luxuries in life. It is primarily concerned with financial abundance, but also affects abundance of happiness and the extra things in life that make us feel good.

Enhance the energy of this zone with a symbol of abundance that is meaningful for you.

SolePath energy tools for intellectuals

Animal instinct	hawk
Trigram of the tao	wind
Colour	purple
Gemstone	amethyst
Essential oil	orange
Feng shui zone	wealth & happiness

Intuitive tools: for our ideas and imagination people who can rely on their gut

Animal instinct = dolphin

Dolphins are able to listen at several different levels simultaneously; they are sensitive, keenly aware of others, live in the now, the present moment, and are playful.

Trigram of the tao = lake

The trigram of lake denotes joy. Lake is contained joy and has depth without overflowing.

Colour = white

White enhances creativity and is the symbol of peace and purity. White creates balance and harmony and it is the colour of awakening and ideas. White can also clear blocks, provide clarity and give a feeling of freedom and openness. When intuitives wear white they connect to their inner child and can more easily trust their instincts and gut feeling.

Gemstone = clear quartz

Clear quartz holds intention and amplifies it. Clear quartz increases imagination, creativity and provides clarity. When intuitives carry clear quartz they are better able to manifest their ideas and know that they are connected to the creative power of our planet earth.

Essential oil = peppermint

Peppermint revives and lifts energy. When intuitives use peppermint they feel a zest for life and know that life is what they make of it.

Dr. Debra Ford Msc.D

<u>Feng shui zone = fun & creativity</u>

The energy for the intuitive SolePaths is found in the fun & creativity zone of a space. The energy of this zone is all about having fun, of being uninhibited and enjoying life — like a child. This Zone contains our creative energy and how we express ourselves.

Enhance the energy of this zone with something that reflects your creative ideas.

SolePath energy tools for intuitives

Animal instinct	dolphin
Trigram of the tao	lake
Colour	white
Gemstone	clear quartz
Essential oil	peppermint
Feng shui zone	fun & creativity

Spiritual tools: for our spiritual explorers who are experiencing 'what you cannot see'

Animal instinct = dog

Dogs serve humanity, they live and work for community, responding to the needs of others; showing love and appreciation for others.

Trigram of the tao = mountain

The trigram mountain denotes constancy. Mountain is everlasting, durable, all seeing and always there.

Colour = blue

Blue is the colour of spiritual connectivity and it allows access to wisdom and guidance. Blue instills faith in self and creates calm and peacefulness. It assists with easy communication and self-expression. When spirituals wear blue they are able to safely explore their connection to 'what you cannot see' and share it with others.

Gemstone = lapis lazuli

Lapis lazuli assists with accessing universal knowledge and enhancing spirituality. When spirituals carry lapis lazuli they feel more connected and at peace.

Essential oil = ylang ylang

Ylang ylang connects you to your true self, your higher self. When spirituals use ylang ylang they find balance and peace.

Dr. Debra Ford Msc.D

Feng shui zone = wisdom & spirituality

The energy for the spiritual SolePaths is found in the wisdom & spirituality zone of a space. The energy of this zone affects our spiritual connection. It is related to our ability to gain wisdom and understanding.

Enhance the energy of this zone with a spiritual image or statue.

SolePath energy tools for Spirituals

Animal instinct	dog
Trigram of the tao	mountain
Colour	blue
Gemstone	lapis Lazuli
Essential oil	ylang ylang
Feng shui zone	wisdom & spirituality

The following energy tools, SolePath, Seth and SolePlan, are available to all 22 SolePaths. Review the energy of each tool to decide if you need it or check in with your pendulum.

SolePath tools: your path to purpose and a beautiful life

Animal instinct = ox

Ox is powerful, protective, determined and resolute; valuing commitment, with an air of nobility.

Trigram of the tao = earth

The trigram earth denotes receptivity. Earth is nourishing, life giving, stable and reliable.

Colour = pink

Pink represents all forms of love; it is a colour that facilitates compassion, tolerance and acceptance. Pink represents yin energy and connection to our planet earth. It is a nurturing, loving and life-giving colour. When you wear pink you heal emotionally and feel calm, tranquil and protected. Pink neutralizes disorder; it helps create peace, assists with relaxation, instills a sense of contentment as you walk your path to purpose.

Gemstone = rose quartz

Rose quartz stimulates unconditional love. Rose quartz heals emotional wounds and encourages deep inner healing. When you carry rose quartz you feel calm, reassured and peaceful. Rose quartz strengthens you as you go with the flow of your life.

Essential oil = juniper berry

Juniper berry enhances love of self and of others. When you use Juniper berry you have inner courage and interact with others in a warm, strong and positive way.

Feng shui zone = love & attraction

The overall energy for SolePath is found in the love & attraction zone of a space. The energy of this zone is all about love. This energy affects two kinds of love — self love (self esteem), how we feel about ourselves; as well as romantic love.

Enhance the energy of this zone with something you feel is symbolic of your SolePath.

SolePath energy tools

Animal instinct	ox
Trigram of the tao	earth
Colour	pink
Gemstone	rose quartz
Essential oil	juniper berry
Feng shui zone	love & attraction

Seth tools: our principle SolePath guide

Animal instinct = horse

Horses place a high priority on personal freedom, live in other dimensions and realities but function well in the practical world. Horses are loyal once trust is earned, natural leaders, evoke confidence in others, and love to wander and explore with no agenda.

Trigram of the tao = heaven

The trigram heaven denotes creativity. Heaven is energetic, changing and expanding.

Colour = silver

Silver has the energy of stillness, warmth and security; it is a colour that represents maturity and dependability. Silver aids communication on both the physical and non-physical plane. It has a soothing and calming influence that puts life experiences into perspective. When you wear silver you feel calm and connected to your inner wisdom. Silver creates independence, self-reliance and courage.

Gemstone = smoky quartz

Smoky quartz assists with spiritual connection. Smoky quartz encourages emotional calmness and relieves fears. When you carry smoky quartz you find it easier to interpret insights from the non-physical realms and to receive inspiration.

Essential oil = myrrh

Myrrh promotes inner peace and tranquility. When you use myrrh you tap into the field and have access to wisdom.

Dr. Debra Ford Msc.D

Feng shui zone = support & guidance

The overall energy for Seth is found in the support & guidance zone of a space. The energy of this zone affects finding people who can help in life. This may be support from physical people; or guidance from non-physical beings — whatever we may call them, angels or spirit guides.

Enhance the energy of this zone with a spiritual image or artifact.

SolePath energy tools for Seth

Animal instinct	horse
Trigram of the tao	heaven
Colour	silver
Gemstone	smoky quartz
Essential oil	myrrh
Feng shui zone	support & guidance

SolePlan tools: the plan for your life

Animal instinct = lion

Lions have a strong life energy, are best when functioning as part of a community, and push self to learn more.

Symbol = yin yang which is all of the trigrams combined

The yin yang denotes balance.

Colour = yellow

Yellow vibrates with the energy of stability and grounding. Yellow encourages happy and optimistic feelings and uplifts the spirits and creates joy. Yellow brings on feelings of living a fulfilled life. When you wear yellow you feel strong, full of life-force and balanced (mentally, physically and spiritually).

Gemstone = citrine

Citrine promotes Joy. Citrine is highly energizing and carries the energy of the sun. When you carry citrine you feel healthy, optimistic, balanced and joyful.

Essential oil = patchouli

Patchouli promotes emotional and mental balance. When you use patchouli you feel more joyful and in the flow of life.

Dr. Debra Ford Msc.D

Feng shui zone = health & joy

The overall energy for SolePlan is found in the health & joy zone of a space. The energy of this zone affects our mental and physical health and when we're healthy we feel great.

Enhance the energy of this zone with your written intentions. If you need guidance on writing intentions refer to my book 'the energy of intention'.

SolePath energy tools for SolePlan

Animal instinct	lion
Trigram of the tao	yin yang
Colour	yellow
Gemstone	citrine
Essential oil	patchouli
Feng shui zone	health & joy

Dr. Debra Ford Msc.D

SECTION 7 – YOUR GREAT TRUTH

Every man or woman who marries into this house, every child, has to put their gifts at its disposal. If we could manage to pool all of that; if we could each do what we can do; then Downton has a real chance.

Downton Abbey, period drama created by Julian Fellowes.

Dr. Debra Ford Msc.D

SECTION 7 – YOUR GREAT TRUTH

If you are feeling that there is something that you were born to do, some way that you were born to serve, this book is for you. I have written it for you and for Caleb who wrote to me

I have always felt this way, always. I have been searching for direction my whole life, not quite feeling the correct fit."

Caleb Lee

Your great truth lies within your gifts and greatness. We are all so familiar with our own characteristics that we often feel that they aren't really anything special; that everyone can do what we do; that who we are isn't unique.

But I know that this is not so.

Each of you has a specific SolePath, a path that is the guide to living the life your soul intended, a path that leads to your life's purpose, to answering the question 'how may I serve'.

In a movie about writers called 'wonder boys' there is a great line that says *'it's like all of your sentences existed, in style, waiting for you to bring them down'*. Your great truth is waiting for you to 'bring it down'.

Here are the agreements I made with myself and with my guides to manifest the SolePath body of work.

- Cultivate an open mind. What you are dreaming about, working with, testing, doesn't have to be logical or someone else's wisdom or scientifically proven or metaphysically already manifest.

- Trust your imagination. Listen to your guides, don't ignore the voice in your head. Make time for quiet and create the opportunity to hear. Yes, you are making it up! Yes, it is all your imagination.

- Follow the next breadcrumb. You don't have to see the whole path. The next step leads to the next step, which leads to your greatness, even if you can't see how. In hindsight I can connect the dots between my great fascination with feng shui, the iching, my doctoral studies and the manifestation of this new body of work called SolePath, but I certainly couldn't see it at the time.

- Record it. Your inspiration, your questions, quotations that catch your eye, your musings and journaling; all of it, all the time. Be prepared, whether it is a notebook, audio recording or digital note.

- Stand tall. Stick your head out of your hole and don't fret about the consequences. Your guides are with you; it is time. I was lucky enough to attend a 'conversations with god' conference in May 2006 and get a private audience with Neale Donald Walsch. He said 'you will stick your head out of the sand and you will get shot at', and he was right. And it has been worth it! I read somewhere that all great teachings are welcomed into the world like a smallpox epidemic

Dr. Debra Ford Msc.D

and we know that every new great creative idea was at sometime just a notion in someone's imagination.

- You matter too. Your purpose is not only manifesting your perfect truth as a teaching, your life is also about having the experience your soul intended. It isn't all about the teachings, it is also about you and your path and having fun.

There is nothing more difficult to take in hand, more perilous to conduct, or more uncertain in its success, than to take the lead in the introduction of a new order to things.

Niccolo Machiavelli

I am so thankful for bringing the SolePath teachings forward, for finding myself in a place where I could hear, for finding myself surrounded by people who are supporting the manifestation of this great work.

I know this for sure, if you live your life in your LightPaths, you are connected to your soul and it is possible for you to navigate towards this great truth that will be the teaching of your life.

You don't have to have any particular SolePath, because when you live your life in your LightPaths, whatever they are, you are connected to your wisdom, to your higher self, to your soul, your guides, your angels, your god. It is from this place of expanded energy that you can hear the wisdom.

This is the timeline for my journey. Be patient with the unfolding of yours.

SolePath
timeline

1957
June 25: Dr. Debra born in durban, south africa.

1971
Motor vehicle accident in kimberley, south africa. A near death
experience, one of Dr. Debra's exit points.

1984
Dr. Debra and John's daughter, Elizabeth, miscarries late in pregnancy.

1990
Dr. Debra, John and sons Joel and Adam immigrate to canada.

1995
Spiritual journey begins with feng shui, dowsing and space clearing.

2003
Feng shui teacher, created college curriculum for feng shui.

September: published first book 'in the feng shui zone, good health,
great relationships, abundant prosperity'.

2006
June: Peter, Dr. Debra's first non-physical guide shows up.
August: during surgery, Dr. Debra introduced to her council of seven;
a group of non-physical beings.
September: Peter leads Dr. Debra through door, promising to
be with her for the whole journey.

2007
Learns that Elizabeth is non-physical guide shepherding souls as they take up
residence in their physical body. Experience as fetus in Dr. Debra's
womb prepared her for this work, her soul's purpose.

September: awarded doctorate in metaphysical science from
university of metaphysics at sedona.

Dr. Debra Ford Msc.D

2009

April: attendance at gateway voyage, one week meditation
intensive at monroe institute.

June 24: meditation evening at John and Dr. Debra's
home, conception of SolePath.

June 25: SolePath birth and two week downloading of this sacred
teaching from Dr. Debra's council of seven.

2011

June: new guide Jane arrives. Appears much bigger than normal sized person and
in a physical body. Sits in chair and peers at Dr. Debra over reading glasses.

September: Seth appears, distinguished looking man, saying
nothing, simply standing comfortably behind Jane's chair.

2012

January: another surgery from same 2006 surgeon. Dr. Debra understands
that it is another exit point, but chooses not to go 'home'.

February 10: burning the 3am oil, written conversations
with Seth and Jane begin.

May 24: prompted by Deneen, first conversation with Seth is recorded.

2013

May 26 to June 1: SolePath book written in hong kong, one of throat
chakras of world, on 27th floor of island pacific hotel.

June 9: Seth explains purpose of SolePath book; inspire others to manifest
their own great truth, so that all may ask 'how may we serve'.

This book is about inspiring you towards your own body of work; the great truth that will be yours. Your LightPaths are how you navigate to your life's purpose and within each LightPath there is direction towards your great truth.

This is living your beautiful life!

Charismatic adventurer

The great truth for a charismatic adventurer is about embracing change; introducing new ideas; new ideas that challenge the status quo.

Spiritual balance

The great truth for a spiritual balance is about flowing downstream; non-resisting; living life in the moment, with grace.

Intuitive builder

The great truth for an intuitive builder is about seeing possibilities; sharing possibilities with others; creating abundance for all.

Compassionate caretaker

The great truth for a compassionate caretaker is about caring for people; caring about people; making others feel better.

Inspirational conformist

The great truth for an inspirational conformist is about valuing tradition; learning from the successes of the past; not forgetting historical lessons.

Dr. Debra Ford Msc.D

Intellectual controller

The great truth for an intellectual controller is about seeing the vision; looking ahead; motivating others to walk the path with you.

Intuitive creator

The great truth for an intuitive creator is about leaving the world more beautiful; manifesting beautiful ideas; creating beautiful experiences.

Intellectual expert

The great truth for an intellectual expert is about specializing; expanding the knowledge base; pushing intellectual boundaries.

Compassionate facilitator

The great truth for a compassionate facilitator is about building community; defining community; caring for community.

Charismatic gladiator

The great truth for a charismatic gladiator is about raising standards; being better; striving for excellence.

Compassionate healer

The great truth for a compassionate healer is about fixing what is broken; identifying what needs to be fixed; knowing what to do.

Inspirational humanitarian

The great truth for an inspirational humanitarian is about standing up for a cause; standing up for those who can't stand up for themselves; creating practical solutions.

Intuitive hunter

The great truth for an intuitive hunter is about seeking and sharing; finding truth and then bringing it back to share with community; trusting intuition.

Charismatic influencer

The great truth for a charismatic influencer is about influencing others for the greater good; collaborating with others, for the good of all.

Intellectual lateral thinker

The great truth for an intellectual lateral thinker is about innovation and ideas; about inventing things and concepts.

Charismatic leader

The great truth for a charismatic leader is about leading others; blazing a trail; leading from the front.

Inspirational manager

The great truth for an inspirational manager is about making things happen; accomplishing and implementing; getting things done.

Dr. Debra Ford Msc.D

Spiritual mystic

The great truth for a spiritual mystic is about non-physical connection; pushing spiritual boundaries; spiritual exploration.

Charismatic performer

The great truth for a charismatic performer is about spreading happiness; entertaining others; making others feel good.

Intuitive solitude

The great truth for an intuitive solitude is about finding quiet; accessing imagination; manifesting ideas.

Inspirational teacher

The great truth for an inspirational teacher is about living an inspiring life; communicating with others.

Spiritual warrior

The great truth for a spiritual warrior is about standing up for something you believe in, a spiritual cause and your psychic connection.

Wow! all of us, living in our light, using our gifts and greatness, asking how may we serve, making a difference in the world.

When we all step into our gifts and greatness who knows what we can accomplish together on our planet. I am ready, are you?

Dr. Debra Ford Msc.D

SECTION 8 – THE SACRED DOWNLOADS

- Charismatic SolePaths
- Compassionate SolePaths
- Inspirational SolePaths
- Intellectual SolePaths
- Intuitive SolePaths
- Spiritual SolePaths

IN SOLEPATH YOU UNCOVER THE PATH TO THE WORK THE PERSON CAME TO EARTH TO DO. BY WORK I DO NOT MEAN THE JOB, I MEAN WHAT THEY CAME TO EARTH TO DO. NOT ONLY FOR THEMSELVES BUT FOR OTHERS. AN INTUITIVE CREATOR CAME TO LIVE A BEAUTIFUL LIFE AND TO CREATE BEAUTY FOR OTHERS. AN INTUITIVE BUILDER CAME TO LIVE WITH ABUNDANCE AND TO CREATE ABUNDANCE FOR OTHERS. AN INTUITIVE SOLITUDE CAME TO ACCESS IMAGINATION AND MANIFEST IMAGINATIVE IDEAS FOR OTHERS TO SHARE. THIS IS THE WE AND THE US.

SETH

SECTION 8 – THE SACRED DOWNLOADS

Charismatic SolePaths

Charismatic adventurer

Charismatic Adventurer LightPath

Charismatics are the world's 'sparkle' people. You simply light up our world. With your outgoing sensing and perception, just like a bat you are able to interpret the returning echoes from life. You respond to people, places and experiences by how you sense the world is responding to you. You use others as a mirror for yourself and have an innate sense of how people are reacting to you. You interpret the returning echoes and reflect back what you sense.

Your ability to judge situations keeps you safe because you are an incredible judge of character and you rarely make mistakes in your assessments. You get into difficulty when you don't trust this or allow the opinions of others to get in the way.

As a charismatic adventurer, you love the new and exciting - new learning, new people, new places, new technology … anything new. You are a non-conformist and a ready – fire – aim person with an inexhaustible energy for life. You are a bit of a risk taker and are warm, affectionate and likeable.

Your core energy as a charismatic adventurer is: loving the new and being at the cutting edge. This core energy represents those positive core values deep within you that create an expansion of your energy; that create positive outcomes.

Being a charismatic adventurer means embracing the new. It

means loving change and being discerning about when you are changing for the sake of change, or when you are embracing change because it is an improvement, a moving forward. You teach us how not to fear change and how to embrace new ideas. You show us that moving forward is fun and that the status quo can be improved upon.

Who am I?

A 'sparkle' SolePath, I respond to the world through my perception of how you respond to me. My sense of self is governed by my interpretation of what you think of me — what I do and who I am.

I have an inexhaustible energy for the 'new', for life and I love to explore. I am a non-conformist and a ready-fire-aim person who loves anything new. I am a risk taker who is outgoing and friendly. I am fun, spontaneous and highly individualistic.

I am warm, affectionate and likeable and have a wide range of friends and associates with whom I feel really at ease. I also make others feel at ease when I am around. I am sensitive and intuitive and can usually read other people and situations. If I don't like what I am sensing, I can become aloof and superior and this makes me feel quite pessimistic.

I am a quick thinker who is always on the lookout for possibilities. I never panic in an emergency, even though I sometimes (deliberately it may seem to others) may endanger myself. Obstacles and danger never deter me; they even sometimes motivate me even further.

I don't like to be told what to do. I don't like bureaucracy and have trouble with rules that don't make sense to me. I feel very grounded and confident in myself.

Dr. Debra Ford Msc.D

What am I doing here?

My Joy comes from discovering new things — new learning, new places, new technology — and I love to talk about what I discover and my exciting experiences. Yes, I may talk too much, but I have many tales of my adventures and lots to say about my experiences. Anyway, my natural talent for language enables me to tell funny stories.

Some may find me impulsive as I can change my focus in an instant (I have a need to explore a wide variety of topics and places), but once I am committed to a course of action I give it my full attention. If I am not fully involved, I have a short attention span, I have trouble following up and become bored very easily.

Charismatic adventurer DarkPath

On the one hand, there is so much about being a charismatic that serves you — you are after all one of the world's 'sparkle' people — and on the other hand there is so much about being a dark charismatic that trips you up.

When you are living your charismatic category from a place of collapsed energy, the overall negative attitude is selfishness and a sense that it really is only about you.

You could easily delight us and light up our world, or use your big energy to shut out the light - even with the full knowing of what the impact is on those around you. You could use your incredible outgoing sensing and perception to amuse and enchant us, or to justify aggressive behaviour towards others.

Yet, when you are experiencing your charismatic category from a place of expanded energy, you contribute to our world with your sparkle, your light and your energy. You are fun and just make us all feel good.

Who is the adventurer?

I am sensitive and intuitive and can usually read other people and situations. If I don't like what I am sensing, I can become aloof and superior and this makes me feel quite pessimistic.

I don't like to be told what to do. I don't like bureaucracy and have trouble with rules that don't make sense to me. I feel very grounded and confident in myself.

Some may find me impulsive as I can change my focus in an

instant (I have a need to explore a wide variety of topics and places), but once I am committed to a course of action I give it my full attention. If I am not fully involved, I have a short attention span, I have trouble following up and become bored very easily.

Who is the DarkPath adventurer?

> The core energy for the dark charismatic adventurer is being a risktaker and gambler. Taking unnecessary risks, whatever the impact on others, whether it be for your safely, your health, in your selection of love partners, or even risking what others have.

I am a reckless risk-taker and will risk everything for a thrill. I am willing to gamble my life and the lives of others; all that I have and all that others have. I don't care about the consequences. I am able to ignore the impact that my risk-taking has on others and persistently seek the unnatural 'high' that I get from living on the edge, whatever the consequences. I don't have a conscience — I don't care what chaos my actions have on the lives of others. I am dangerous as I use my charisma to talk others into forgiving me, so that I can risk them and what they have over and over again.

Other negative characteristics:

I see others as pawns in my own life (what can I get from you). When you are no longer useful to me I discard you. I am disconnected from the feelings of others and use words as weapons to get my own way. I am inconsistent which makes me unable to see things through.

Charismatic gladiator

Charismatic gladiator LightPath

Charismatics are the world's 'sparkle' people. You simply light up our world. With your outgoing sensing and perception, just like a bat you are able to interpret the returning echoes from life. You respond to people, places and experiences by how you sense the world is responding to you. You use others as a mirror for yourself and have an innate sense of how people are reacting to you. You interpret the returning echoes and reflect back what you sense.

Your ability to judge situations keeps you safe because you are an incredible judge of character and you rarely make mistakes in your assessments. You get into difficulty when you don't trust this or allow the opinions of others to get in the way.

As a charismatic gladiator, you raise the bar; you push us to higher standards. You are motivated by competition and raise the standards of performance of all of us. You love excitement and are always on the look out for an opportunity to win. You have a deep belief in yourself and your innate skills.

Your core energy as a charismatic gladiator is: excellence and raising the Bar. This core energy represents those positive core values deep within you that create an expansion of your energy; that create positive outcomes.

Being a charismatic gladiator means always striving for a better standard, pushing the rest of us to a higher standard of excellence, always raising the bar. You just want to be better and love a competitive environment. You just sense that it could be better!

Dr. Debra Ford Msc.D

Who am I?

A 'sparkle' SolePath, I respond to the world through my perception of how you respond to me. My sense of self is governed by my interpretation of what you think of me — what I do and who I am.

I love to win! I am first and foremost a competitor who is persevering, dedicated and hardworking. I love showing my skills and don't mind being the centre of attention.

At my best I am competitive, fair and focused. On a bad day I am all about winning no matter how I do it, and I don't mind stretching the rules to get what I want — a win. Some may feel that this makes me ruthless and arrogant; I certainly can have a killer instinct when I want to win and my arrogance comes from my deep belief in myself and my innate skills.

I play hard and I work hard and I am motivated by competition. I need to take care that my competitive instincts are tempered in my relationships with those I love.

What am I doing here?

My Joy comes from my desire to win, to raise the bar for all those against whom I compete. Faster, better, more efficient, more cost effective, more attractive, simpler, funnier — you name it I raise the standards of performance.

I sign up for jobs that most others wouldn't even consider. Anything that involves excitement, risk, and winning! In the olden days I probably would have been a gladiator, a medieval knight, a mercenary or a pirate always looking for an opportunity to win! I work best alone, love the new and exciting; I am just not made for the quiet life.

Charismatic gladiator DarkPath

On the one hand, there is so much about being a charismatic that serves you — you are after all one of the world's 'sparkle' people — and on the other hand there is so much about being a dark charismatic that trips you up.

When you are living your charismatic category from a place of collapsed energy, the overall negative attitude is selfishness and a sense that it really is only about you.

You could easily delight us and light up our world, or use your big energy to shut out the light - even with the full knowing of what the impact is on those around you. You could use your incredible outgoing sensing and perception to amuse and enchant us, or to justify aggressive behaviour towards others.

Yet, when you are experiencing your charismatic category from a place of expanded energy, you contribute to our world with your sparkle, your light and your energy. You are fun and just make us all feel good.

Who is the gladiator?

At my best I am competitive, fair and focused. On a bad day I am all about winning no matter how I do it, and I don't mind stretching the rules to get what I want — a win. Some may feel that this makes me ruthless and arrogant; I certainly can have a killer instinct when I want to win and my arrogance comes from my deep belief in myself and my innate skills.

Dr. Debra Ford Msc.D

Who is the DarkPath gladiator?

> The core energy for the dark charismatic gladiator is being ruthless and winning at all costs. Stretching the rules to get what you want, which is a win. Having a killer instinct and a deep feeling of superiority.

In all parts of my life, I will cheat, lie and steal - to win. I have very loose morality and there are no rules for me when it comes to me getting my 'win', getting my own way. I can charm you with my deceptive smile, but know that if you try to get in my way I will mow you down. You won't get in my way, I won't allow it — I intimidate you with my loudness - I talk too loudly, joke too loudly and use this to mask a deep feeling of superiority towards you.

Other negative characteristics:

I work best alone and am really frustrated by your interference; after all you are inferior to me. I cannot settle down and have a need for excitement all the time.

Charismatic influencer

Charismatic influencer LightPath

Charismatics are the world's 'sparkle' people. You simply light up our world. With your outgoing sensing and perception, just like a bat you are able to interpret the returning echoes from life. You respond to people, places and experiences by how you sense the world is responding to you. You use others as a mirror for yourself and have an innate sense of how people are reacting to you. You interpret the returning echoes and reflect back what you sense.

Your ability to judge situations keeps you safe because you are an incredible judge of character and you rarely make mistakes in your assessments. You get into difficulty when you don't trust this or allow the opinions of others to get in the way.

As a charismatic influencer, you influence us toward the greater good. You are an in charge person who is inspiring. You are believable and have the gift of the gab and are interested in, know and understand people. Your personal goals are for the greater good and you need to be independent.

Your core energy as a charismatic influencer is: encouraging collaboration and influencing for the greater good. This core energy represents those positive core values deep within you that create an expansion of your energy; that create positive outcomes.

Being a charismatic influencer means that you understand how to get people to work with you to achieve your intentions. You are a great motivator when convincing others to work with you and you deeply understand collaboration.

Dr. Debra Ford Msc.D

Who am I?

A 'Sparkle' SolePath, I respond to the world through my perception of how you respond to me. My sense of self is governed by my interpretation of what you think of me — what I do and who I am.

I am called to get others to work with me to achieve my intentions for the greater good. I am called to inspire others to achieve goals that will make the world a better place for us all. I live in a world of exciting possibilities and can accomplish anything that captivates my interest. When I get excited, people get excited and work with me to achieve my goals. I am always able to persuade the right people to support my intentions. I am an in-charge person who is very believable and has the gift of the gab. To some, I may seem self-centered and manipulative as I can play any role to get what I want.

I know people, I understand people, I am interested in people. I have an exceptional ability to intuitively understand others in a very short space of time. I look at others and know how they can help me achieve my intentions.

I have a strong need to be independent and maintain control over my life. That's why I am better in my own business where I can decide what I will work on, rather than as an employee doing what others tell me to do. Some may feel that I have difficulty completing projects but when I lose interest it is impossible for me to stay involved.

I also need time alone to make sure that I am moving in the right direction. I only feel good when I am living an authentic life in line with my strong set of values.

What am I doing here?

My Joy comes from inspiring people to help me realize my intentions, which I believe are for the greater good of society.

I have a considerable intellect that I use to influence others. I am a respected member of my community; people look up to me and seek out my opinions and my support.

Dr. Debra Ford Msc.D

Charismatic influencer DarkPath

On the one hand, there is so much about being a charismatic that serves you — you are after all one of the world's 'sparkle' people — and on the other hand there is so much about being a dark charismatic that trips you up.

When you are living your charismatic category from a place of collapsed energy, the overall negative attitude is selfishness and a sense that it really is only about you.

You could easily delight us and light up our world, or use your big energy to shut out the light - even with the full knowing of what the impact is on those around you. You could use your incredible outgoing sensing and perception to amuse and enchant us, or to justify aggressive behaviour towards others.

Yet, when you are experiencing your charismatic category from a place of expanded energy, you contribute to our world with your sparkle, your light and your energy. You are fun and just make us all feel good.

Who is the influencer?

I am always able to persuade the right people to support my intentions. To some, I may seem self-centered and manipulative as I can play any role to get what I want.

I have a strong need to be independent and maintain control over my life. That's why I am better in my own business where I can decide what I will work on, rather than as an employee doing what others tell me to do. Some may feel that I have difficulty completing projects but when I lose interest it is impossible for me to stay involved. I have a considerable intellect that I use to influence others.

Who is the DarkPath influencer?

> The core energy for the dark charismatic influencer is manipulating to get what you want. Being self-centred and using others as pawns to achieve your own goals. Feeling that the rules don't apply to you.

I am a manipulator and use whatever means is at my disposal to get others to do what I want. I will use emotional blackmail, deception, bullying – I don't care what it takes to get others to do my bidding. I only view them as pawns in my chess game – what can they do to help me achieve my ultimate prize? I have very loose morals and certainly don't think that the rules that others play by have anything to do with me. I don't really think that it is lying if it helps me achieve my intentions.

Other negative characteristics:

I have a short attention span, am impatient and easily get irritable with those around me. Don't feel that you are my friend – when your usefulness is over, so is our relationship.

Dr. Debra Ford Msc.D

Charismatic leader

Charismatic leader LightPath

Charismatics are the world's 'sparkle' people. You simply light up our world. With your outgoing sensing and perception, just like a bat you are able to interpret the returning echoes from life. You respond to people, places and experiences by how you sense the world is responding to you. You use others as a mirror for yourself and have an innate sense of how people are reacting to you. You interpret the returning echoes and reflect back what you sense.

Your ability to judge situations keeps you safe because you are an incredible judge of character and you rarely make mistakes in your assessments. You get into difficulty when you don't trust this or allow the opinions of others to get in the way.

As a charismatic leader, you show others the way by your example. You are charismatic, believable and fun to be around. Your excitement about life is infectious. You understand people, their attitudes and motivation and have an incredible ability to think on your feet.

Your core energy as a charismatic leader is: leading others and sparkle and charisma. This core energy represents those positive core values deep within you that create an expansion of your energy; that create positive outcomes.

Being a charismatic leader means being born to lead – you simply gather a crowd. A bit like the movie character Forest Gump who decided to run and turned around to find that he had gathered a big following. They didn't know why he was running, or where he was going – but they simply felt drawn to follow him. That's a born leader.

Who am I?

A 'sparkle' SolePath, I respond to the world through my perception of how you respond to me. My sense of self is governed by my interpretation of what you think of me — what I do and who I am.

Mine is the charismatic SolePath. I get excited about life; I get others excited about life and lead from the front. I am charismatic and can usually sell anyone my ideas. I have an extraordinary talent for getting things started, but am not so good with the follow-through.

I understand people and have the ability to understand their attitudes and motivations. I suppose I read people like a book and am typically a couple of steps ahead of them. I may sometimes stretch the rules to get things done; anyway I feel most of those rules do nothing for society.

I move fast, I talk fast, I have style and love the good things in life. I don't always have a plan, I think on my feet and usually achieve what I want to. I am a good decision maker who likes to get things done — I get really impatient with what seems to be irrelevant theory.

I love to have fun and don't shy away from the limelight. I get bored easily in my work and home life, and need to keep moving. I hate being restricted or confined.

What am I doing here?

My Joy comes from being a leader of society. I show others the way and lead by example. People find me charismatic, believable and look up to me. People follow me; I just seem to gather a crowd.

Dr. Debra Ford Msc.D

I have found that I have been 'leading' others since I can remember. From an early age I have found myself in charge of others and have often wondered how it happened. It just comes naturally to me to be the leader and get others to follow me.

I have no difficulty looking at the facts, quickly deciding what needs to be done and then moving forward.

Charismatic leader DarkPath

On the one hand, there is so much about being a charismatic that serves you — you are after all one of the world's 'sparkle' people — and on the other hand there is so much about being a dark charismatic that trips you up.

When you are living your charismatic category from a place of collapsed energy, the overall negative attitude is selfishness and a sense that it really is only about you.

You could easily delight us and light up our world, or use your big energy to shut out the light - even with the full knowing of what the impact is on those around you. You could use your incredible outgoing sensing and perception to amuse and enchant us, or to justify aggressive behaviour towards others.

Yet, when you are experiencing your charismatic category from a place of expanded energy, you contribute to our world with your sparkle, your light and your energy. You are fun and just make us all feel good.

Who is the leader?

I understand people and have the ability to understand their attitudes and motivations. I may sometimes stretch the rules to get things done; anyway I feel most of those rules do nothing for society. I have an extraordinary talent for getting things started, but am not so good with the follow-through. I don't always have a plan, I think on my feet and usually achieve what I want to. I am a good decision maker who likes to get things done — I get really impatient with what seems to be irrelevant theory

I get bored easily in my work and home life, and need to

Dr. Debra Ford Msc.D

keep moving. I hate being restricted or confined.

Who is the DarkPath leader?

> The core energy for the dark charismatic leader is leading others astray. Feeling that it is their fault if they follow you and not really caring where they end up. Stretching the rules and not really thinking things through.

It is your problem if you 'follow' me and then don't like where you end up. I didn't ask you to follow me (although I certainly did encourage it) and if you end up somewhere that doesn't make you feel comfortable, I will abandon you and move on to find other 'stooges' to lead. I don't care if I lead you astray and don't care about the wreckage I leave in my wake; I am only interested in 'number one'.

Other negative characteristics:

I don't usually finish what I start as I get bored easily. You may just be getting excited about where I am leading you and I will move onto another plan. I am a fast talker, who doesn't think things through and why should I – I get people to follow me anyway.

Charismatic performer

Charismatic performer LightPath

Charismatics are the world's 'sparkle' people. You simply light up our world. With your outgoing sensing and perception, just like a bat you are able to interpret the returning echoes from life. You respond to people, places and experiences by how you sense the world is responding to you. You use others as a mirror for yourself and have an innate sense of how people are reacting to you. You interpret the returning echoes and reflect back what you sense.

Your ability to judge situations keeps you safe because you are an incredible judge of character and you rarely make mistakes in your assessments. You get into difficulty when you don't trust this or allow the opinions of others to get in the way.

As a charismatic performer, the world is your stage. You love the limelight and being recognized and admired for your talent. You really must have an audience and are spontaneous and fun-loving. You love sensation and drama and have the great gift of living in the moment.

Your core energy as a charismatic performer is: performing and entertaining and being an extrovert. This core energy represents those positive core values deep within you that create an expansion of your energy; that create positive outcomes.

Being a charismatic performer means that you understand that your life is a movie and you have the ability to rewrite the script at any moment. You do love to be the lead actor and direct your supporting cast and entertain your audience. You are really fun to be around.

Who am I?

A 'sparkle' SolePath, I respond to the world through my perception of how you respond to me. My sense of self is governed by my interpretation of what you think of me — what I do and who I am.

My SolePath is all about 'me'! I love the limelight and being admired for my talent. I like to be the centre of attention and only feel alive when I have an audience — even if it is only one person.

I am spontaneous and I know how to have fun. I am always upbeat and can lift the spirits of anyone. I am a very warm person and treat everyone as if they were my best friend (now you know why I was the most popular person at school).

I can be dedicated to my talent because I understand that this is why people admire me.

I love people and with my strong interpersonal skills will talk to anyone. I love new experiences, including conversations with new people, and can make them feel like they are the most important person in the world to me at that moment. I love sensation and drama. In fact I love to have people around me all the time.

I feel quite stressed and unhappy when I am isolated from people and when I have too much time to think I become quite morose. I live in the moment and want to be performing every single minute. I live a fast paced life and I am always on the go and need lots of diversity.

What am I doing here? My Joy comes from creating joy for others when I perform. The entire world is my stage and I am very good at putting on a show for others. I bring beauty to the world and I love natural beauty.

Charismatic performer DarkPath

On the one hand, there is so much about being a charismatic that serves you — you are after all one of the world's 'sparkle' people — and on the other hand there is so much about being a dark charismatic that trips you up.

When you are living your charismatic category from a place of collapsed energy, the overall negative attitude is selfishness and a sense that it really is only about you.

You could easily delight us and light up our world, or use your big energy to shut out the light - even with the full knowing of what the impact is on those around you. You could use your incredible outgoing sensing and perception to amuse and enchant us, or to justify aggressive behaviour towards others.

Yet, when you are experiencing your charismatic category from a place of expanded energy, you contribute to our world with your sparkle, your light and your energy. You are fun and just make us all feel good.

Who is the performer?

My SolePath is all about 'me'! I love the limelight and being admired for my talent. I like to be the centre of attention and only feel alive when I have an audience — even if it is only one person.

I feel quite stressed and unhappy when I am isolated from people and when I have too much time to think I become quite morose. I live in the moment and want to be performing every single minute. I live a fast paced life and I am always on the go and need lots of diversity.

Dr. Debra Ford Msc.D

Who is the DarkPath performer?

> The core energy for the dark charismatic performer is being a selfish drama queen. Feeling that life is all about you, that you are the star of the show and creating drama wherever you go.

I am selfish, I must be the star of the show and you are only important to me if you are part of my supporting cast or in the audience. The world is my stage and I am definitely the lead actor. I create drama everywhere I go, in all my relationships, in all my interactions, as it allows me to be centre stage. I lack compassion and don't care about the impact of my dramas. I am unkind to others, if they don't play their part in supporting me — the person around whom the world turns.

Other negative characteristics:

I need an audience all the time; I need people around me, adoring and admiring me all the time. I easily plunge into sadness or depression but you will never know if it is real or just another drama that I am acting out. If you decide not to be in my supporting cast or my appreciative audience, I will probably turn on you and create negative drama.

Compassionate SolePaths

Compassionate caretaker

Compassionate caretaker LightPath

Compassionates are the 'love' SolePaths. You respond to the world through your heart feeling. As a compassionate, you can absolutely trust your heart and when you do trust your positive emotions, you can be certain of a good outcome, situation or decision.

Your heart keeps you safe because when you clearly identify whether you are feeling 'good' or 'bad' about someone or something, you don't make mistakes. You get into difficulty when you don't trust this, or allow the opinions of others to get in the way.

As a compassionate caretaker, you happily care for others and are sympathetic, helpful and co-operative. You love people and love to be liked. You are extremely reliable, highly co-operative and a great team player. You are trusted.

Your core energy as a compassionate caretaker is: feeling compassion and loving people. This core energy represents those positive core values deep within you that create an expansion of your energy; that create positive, loving feelings.

Being a compassionate caretaker means loving humanity, loving other people and loving yourself too. It means being gentle on others and yourself and participating in the world with compassion. The interaction that brings you the most joy and peace and a feeling of being on purpose, is connecting with people in a loving way.

Dr. Debra Ford Msc.D

Who am I?

I respond to the world through my heart. I can trust my feelings. When I identify whether I am feeling 'good' or 'bad', I don't make mistakes. I get into difficulty when I don't trust this and over think, or allow the opinions of others to get in the way.

Mine is a 'love' SolePath. I care about everyone. I am popular and this is probably because of my special gift of making others feel good about themselves. I get a lot of satisfaction from the happiness of others and seem to be able to bring out the best in them. I am sympathetic, helpful, co-operative and sometimes take on the issues of those I am interacting with. I love other people and hearing their stories. I do love to be liked and this often makes it difficult for me to see the truth about others.

My friends are very important to me and I love to have people over and make sure that they enjoy themselves. I especially enjoy it when we reminisce about good times from the past, but I need to watch myself sometimes as I can participate in and share gossip. I am sensitive to how others are feeling and good at understanding their point of view.

I am loving, supportive and unfailingly generous with my time, my talent and my energy. I do need to hear 'thank-you' from those I care for, and am sometimes resentful of being taken for granted. I need to let go of wanting this appreciation, as I feel so much happier when I remember that I am doing it because it is who I am.

I have a big ego, but often need approval from others to feel good about myself and need to work on my strong reaction to personal criticism. I do get hurt by unkindness, I don't understand it at all and it makes me feel that the world is a dangerous place.

What am I doing here?

My Joy comes from happily giving my time and energy to make sure the needs of others are met. I just seem to know what needs to be done to help even before those needing care realize it. You can always rely on me, if I say that I will do something or be somewhere, know that it will be so. I am highly co-operative and a great team player, although I do like to have some measure of control. People trust me because I am down-to-earth and consistent.

Dr. Debra Ford Msc.D

Compassionate caretaker DarkPath

On the one hand, there is so much about being a compassionate that serves you — you are after all one of the world's most loving people, with a big heart — and on the other hand there is so much about being a dark compassionate that trips you up.

When you are experiencing your compassionate category from a place of collapsed energy, the overall negative attitude is a victim mentality. You give and give to others and then feel taken advantage of; you do not set boundaries and then complain of being taken for granted. People really don't know how to interact with you or where they stand with you.

You are not the best judge of character and often make mistakes with people, either of the heart, or in business dealings. Because of this, you are fearful that something will always go wrong and this fear is generally what causes things to go wrong.

Yet, when you are experiencing your compassionate category from a place of expanded energy, your love and your big heart just make us feel wonderful.

Who is the caretaker?

I am loving, supportive and unfailingly generous with my time, my talent and my energy. I do need to hear 'thank-you' from those I care for, and am sometimes resentful of being taken for granted.

I have a big ego, but often need approval from others to feel good about myself and need to work on my strong reaction to personal criticism. I do get hurt by unkindness, I don't understand it at all and it makes me feel that the world is a dangerous place.

I am sympathetic, helpful, co-operative and sometimes take on the issues of those I am interacting with. I do love to be liked and this often makes it difficult for me to see the truth about others. I need to watch myself sometimes as I can participate in and share gossip.

Who is the DarkPath caretaker?

> The core energy for the dark compassionate caretaker is being a victim. Overreacting to perceived personal criticism and feeling that you never receive enough thanks.

I am a victim. Everyone always takes advantage of me and I never get enough thanks for what I do. I am a difficult friend, partner and co-worker as my need to keep score poisons all of my relationships (if I do this, you need to do that; if I do two things, you need to do two back). My love for others is given and then withheld at a moments notice. You may never know why I no longer love you; you may never know what you did that caused me to declare myself taken advantage of; that caused me to declare myself a victim at your hands.

Other negative characteristics:

My deep desire to be liked makes me a chameleon in my relationships as I try to mould myself to what I think you want — I then resent you for 'making' me do this. I hate you when you point this out to me and then I spread lies and malicious gossip about you.

Dr. Debra Ford Msc.D

Compassionate facilitator

Compassionate facilitator LightPath

Compassionates are the 'love' SolePaths. You respond to the world through your heart feeling. As a compassionate, you can absolutely trust your heart and when you do trust your positive emotions, you can be certain of a good outcome, situation or decision.

Your heart keeps you safe because when you clearly identify whether you are feeling 'good' or 'bad' about someone or something, you don't make mistakes. You get into difficulty when you don't trust this, or allow the opinions of others to get in the way.

As a compassionate facilitator, you are all about community. Once you have enfolded others into your community, your joy comes from being of service to them. You love your community, your family and your cultural traditions. You are loyal to a fault and are a sincere and sympathetic person. You are also responsible, reliable and hard working. To be part of a Facilitator's community and to be loved by a Facilitator is a gift indeed!

Your core energy as a compassionate facilitator is: desire to be of service and love of my community. This core energy represents those positive core values deep within you that create an expansion of your energy; that create positive, loving feelings.

Being a compassionate facilitator means creating community wherever you go and loving and being of service to this community. It means participating in the lives of your community — your family and friends — and creating meaningful relationships. The interaction that brings you the most joy and peace and a feeling of being on purpose, is connecting with the people you love.

Who am I?

I respond to the world through my heart. I can trust my feelings. When I identify whether I am feeling 'good' or 'bad', I don't make mistakes. I get into difficulty when I don't trust this and over think, or allow the opinions of others to get in the way.

I just really, really love my community, my family and friends. My world revolves around those I care about; my joy comes from being of service to them. I am responsible, reliable and strong; I am a hard worker, personable and loyal to a fault. I have a big heart and am sincere and sympathetic.

Sometimes I have difficulty distinguishing between someone who is worth 'following' and supporting and someone who isn't worthy of my trust. My extraordinary loyalty can be taken advantage of and it is best for me to trust the instincts of those I love under these circumstances.

I love the traditions of life, both family traditions and cultural traditions, and I cherish my family, its history and its place in the community. I make it a point to get to know my community and I love chatting with the neighbours!.

As far as money goes, I need to know that I have something put away for a rainy day; it gives me peace of mind to know that the future is taken care of financially. Otherwise I can worry about money and seem a bit 'mean'.

What am I doing here?

My Joy comes from being of service to those I care about. The whole purpose of my existence revolves around my family, my friends and my co-workers. I help my loved ones accomplish their intentions and am often described as 'the

Dr. Debra Ford Msc.D

wind beneath their wings'. I sometimes forget that all those I love are here to have their own experiences and I just want to do it all for them — to protect them from the harsh realities of the world. I willingly work long hours doing tasks that others may find thankless, but I can see that these tasks need to be done and I am quite happy with being the one to do it. I enjoy working alone and rather than delegate or get any help I usually like to do the work myself. I will do whatever it takes to get the task done — I'll move mountains if necessary.

Compassionate facilitator DarkPath

On the one hand, there is so much about being a compassionate that serves you — you are after all one of the world's most loving people, with a big heart — and on the other hand there is so much about being a dark compassionate that trips you up.

When you are experiencing your compassionate category from a place of collapsed energy, the overall negative attitude is a victim mentality. You give and give to others and then feel taken advantage of; you do not set boundaries and then complain of being taken for granted. People really don't know how to interact with you or where they stand with you.

You are not the best judge of character and often make mistakes with people, either of the heart, or in business dealings. Because of this, you are fearful that something will always go wrong and this fear is generally what causes things to go wrong.

Yet, when you are experiencing your compassionate category from a place of expanded energy, your love and your big heart just makes us feel wonderful.

Who is the facilitator?

I just really, really love my community, my family and friends. Sometimes I have difficulty distinguishing between someone who is worth 'following' and supporting and someone who isn't worthy of my trust. My extraordinary loyalty can be taken advantage of and it is best for me to trust the instincts of those I love under these circumstances. I sometimes forget that all those I love are here to have their own experiences and I just want to do it all for them — to protect them from the harsh realities of the world.

Dr. Debra Ford Msc.D

As far as money goes, I need to know that I have something put away for a rainy day; it gives me peace of mind to know that the future is taken care of financially. Otherwise I can worry about money and seem a bit 'mean'.

Who is the DarkPath facilitator?

> The core energy for the dark compassionate facilitator is having a 'sheep mentality'. Following blindly and being easily lead astray. Sometimes being a poor judge of character and then being unable to listen to reason when this is pointed out to you.

I give my loyalty to someone I perceive as being a leader, follow them blindly and will do whatever they ask of me. If I am following you, I don't judge you or your motives and am therefore easily led astray. I will do your dirty work, simply because you ask me to. I am the prototype 'hit man' in the mafia gang – I don't mind doing the deed, I have little or no moral conscience. I simply do it because you asked me to and I am your subject. I am unable to listen to reason, once I have decided to give you my loyalty.

Other negative characteristics:

I am conflicted about money. If you are in my circle of friends and family I am unfailingly generous, but never with those I don't know. Although I won't listen to reason about my own life, I get in the way of others experiences, and interfere in all aspects of the lives of family members because I know best.

Compassionate healer

Compassionate healer LightPath

Compassionates are the 'love' SolePaths. You respond to the world through your heart feeling. As a compassionate, you can absolutely trust your heart and when you do trust your positive emotions, you can be certain of a good outcome, situation or decision.

Your heart keeps you safe because when you clearly identify whether you are feeling 'good' or 'bad' about someone or something, you don't make mistakes. You get into difficulty when you don't trust this, or allow the opinions of others to get in the way.

As a compassionate healer, you care about all living things and have a deep desire to help alleviate pain and suffering and bring wholeness and health to the world. You know how to 'fix' what is broken in our world; once you have decided what it is that you would like to heal — you know how to take the steps to do this. You have a very clear sense of right and wrong, you follow your heart not your head and are willing to make sacrifices for what you believe in.

Your core energy as a compassionate healer is: healing people, animals or the planet and fixing what is wrong. This core energy represents those positive core values deep within you that create an expansion of your energy; that create positive, loving feelings.

Being a compassionate healer means choosing what it is that you would like to heal and then taking action towards that. What you 'fix' will be aligned with your personal beliefs and it could involve people, animals or our planet. The interaction that brings you the most joy and peace and a feeling of being on purpose, is connecting with all living things in a loving way.

Dr. Debra Ford Msc.D

Who am I?

I respond to the world through my heart. I can trust my feelings. When I identify whether I am feeling 'good' or 'bad', I don't make mistakes. I get into difficulty when I don't trust this and over think, or allow the opinions of others to get in the way.

I am a person who cares deeply about all living things and wants to bring wholeness and health to the world. I have a clear sense of right and wrong and see the world as a positive and wonderful place. My deep commitment to the positive and good is boundless.

I 'fix' what is broken. This can be hard for me at times, as it requires me to notice what is wrong with the world, so that I can get involved in repairing it. It is best (for my sanity!) that I don't get involved in the news media, or others stories about catastrophe.

I am patient and welcome new ideas, but am impatient with routine. I work well alone and I work well with people; I follow my heart not my head when making decisions. I am very unsettled by disharmony in my own life and put a great deal of effort into having things run smoothly.

I admit that sometimes I 'heal' what doesn't need to be healed and need to respect boundaries. This interfering only comes from a real desire to heal – even when self-healing is the appropriate course of action.

What am I doing here?

My Joy comes from helping to alleviate pain and suffering and bring wholeness and health to all living things.

I am driven by a strong desire to contribute to the welfare of all living things. I make a conscious and deep commitment to the 'good' of the world and am willing to make sacrifices for what I believe in.

Dr. Debra Ford Msc.D

Compassionate healer DarkPath

On the one hand, there is so much about being a compassionate that serves you — you are after all one of the world's most loving people, with a big heart — and on the other hand there is so much about being a dark compassionate that trips you up.

When you are experiencing your compassionate category from a place of collapsed energy, the overall negative attitude is a victim mentality. You give and give to others and then feel taken advantage of; you do not set boundaries and then complain of being taken for granted. People really don't know how to interact with you or where they stand with you.

You are not the best judge of character and often make mistakes with people, either of the heart, or in business dealings. Because of this, you are fearful that something will always go wrong and this fear is generally what causes things to go wrong.

Yet, when you are experiencing your compassionate category from a place of expanded energy, your love and your big heart just makes us feel wonderful.

Who is the healer?

I am patient and welcome new ideas, but am impatient with routine. I am very unsettled by disharmony in my own life and put a great deal of effort into having things run smoothly.

I admit that sometimes I 'heal' what doesn't need to be healed and need to respect boundaries. This interfering only comes from a real desire to heal — even when self healing is the appropriate course of action.

Who is the DarkPath healer?

> The core energy for the dark compassionate healer is blaming yourself and feeling responsible for all of the bad things that happen around you. You feel constantly criticized and never feel good enough.

I blame myself for everything that goes on in my life and see myself as responsible for everything. This incredible arrogance, of feeling that I am responsible for everything going on around me, is part of my ego. An ego that I pretend is self-deprecating, but in actual fact is an enormous ego that thinks that I am so important that I am at the centre of everything.

I feel others are criticizing me and that I am being judged and found wanting. I criticize myself — for what I do and for who I am — never good enough.

Other negative characteristics:

Cannot cope with disharmony — even the little arguments and disputes become larger than life dramas. I interfere in the lives of others, under the guise of wanting to help but actually because I think that I am the only one who can 'heal' the situation.

Dr. Debra Ford Msc.D

Inspirational SolePaths

Inspirational conformist

Inspirational conformist LightPath

Inspirationals are the world's role models. You respond to the world by wanting to fill a perceived need. As an inspirational, you ask, "What does the world need and how can I provide it?" and "What do you need, and how can I help?"

You have an innate sense of responsibility to yourself, to others and to community, and look at what is needed by both individuals and the group at large. Inspirational SolePaths have the same role as the bones of the body; you provide the structure, the skeleton, the framework for society.

This does not mean that your own needs are lost in your desire to serve, but rather that through your personal learning and experience you feel great empathy with the needs of others and then take action. You inspire us by the way you live your own life and you have a great capacity for getting things done to help others.

As an inspirational conformist the greatest gift that you share with us is your ability to build on what has gone before. Whether it is physical or metaphysical, you have this uncanny ability to see what has gone wrong and what has been extraordinary. You help us create more of what is positive and good, while not repeating the errors of the past. You make sure that the benefits of time honoured traditions are not lost. You have a great sense of right and wrong, are a dependable straight talker who is down to earth and responsible.

Your core energy as an inspirational conformist is: valuing

tradition and cultivating order. This core energy represents those positive core values deep within you that create an expansion of your energy; that create inspiring outcomes.

Being an inspirational conformist means building on what has gone before, not losing what has been great about the past, not rejecting proven traditions. You really understand 'not throwing the baby out with the bath water' and are able to see what has worked before and what will provide a firm foundation for the future.

Who am I?

I respond to the world through my perception of what I think is needed by the group at large. What do you need and how can I help? Inspirational SolePaths have a deep sense of responsibility to the community and are role models for others.

I love traditions and the 'tried and true'. Some may see this as being 'closed' to new ideas but I see it as honouring what has gone before and what has worked before. I like things to be as they are, familiar and ordered. I just prefer the traditional to the new. I don't 'rock the boat' and do have a desire to fit in; I like others to make an effort to conform too.

Even though I may not set the rules, I follow them as I understand that this is for the greater good of us all. I feel really good when people know their duties, follow the guidelines and operate within the rules — and this is how I live my life.

I am very dependable — my words and actions are always a match and you will always know where you stand with me. I am a straight talker (I use my words wisely) and prefer to deal

Dr. Debra Ford Msc.D

only with the facts. I am down to earth, patient with procedures and responsible to a fault.

I may be considered judgmental and lacking in emotion, but I am simply frustrated by the inconsistencies of others. I am highly sociable in small familiar groups but it takes me time to warm up and I do find that emotional interactions leave me feeling exhausted.

What am I doing here?

My Joy comes from making sure that the benefits of time-honoured values and traditions are not lost; if it's not broken, then it probably works!

I have a great sense of right and wrong and willingly participate in keeping societal order. I see the law and tradition as making the world a better place. My perfect profession includes being a referee. I am a true guardian of the institution and am drawn to the service of these institutions. I may be considered intolerant and hard-hearted when dealing with those who don't follow the rules.

Inspirational conformist DarkPath

On the one hand, there is so much about being an inspirational that serves you — you are after all one of the world's role models — and on the other hand there is so much about being a dark inspirational that trips you up.

When you are experiencing your inspirational category from a place of collapsed energy, the overall negative attitude is entitlement and a demand that others obey you. You feel that you are the only one who sees what the world needs and you are certain that your opinions are the only ones that are right. (Even you can see that this is not possible.)

You are intolerant and demand that others look up to you and in the same breath, when you aren't obeyed, complain that you get no support. It must be a throw over from a past life when others were compelled to obey you. Seriously!

Yet, when you are experiencing your inspirational category from a place of expanded energy, you are pretty amazing as you have this deep desire to work towards making a difference in the world.

Who is the conformist?

I am very dependable — my words and actions are always a match and you will always know where you stand with me. I may be considered judgmental and lacking in emotion, but I am simply frustrated by the inconsistencies of others. I am highly sociable in small familiar groups but it takes me time to warm up and I do find that emotional interactions leave me feeling exhausted.

I love traditions and the 'tried and true'. Some may see this as being 'closed' to new ideas but I see it as honouring what

Dr. Debra Ford Msc.D

has gone before and what has worked before. I like things to be as they are, familiar and ordered. I just prefer the traditional to the new. I don't 'rock the boat' and do have a desire to fit in; I like others to make an effort to conform too. I am a true guardian of the Institution and am drawn to the service of these Institutions. I may be considered intolerant and hard-hearted when dealing with those who don't follow the rules. I have a great sense of right and wrong and willingly participate in keeping societal order. I see the law and tradition as making the world a better place.

Who is the DarkPath conformist?

The core energy for the dark inspirational conformist is being hard hearted. Having an intolerant attitude when demanding that others conform to your paradigm, being closed to new ideas and lacking in emotion.

I am intolerant and a hard-hearted bigot. I am hostile to those of differing race, ethnicity, nationality, sexual orientation, various mental disorders, or religion. I won't tolerate you and your differences and your customs. It is your fault you weren't born like me and I don't care that there is no logic to that conclusion. Just follow my rules (revere, respect and look up to me even though I will never return the favour) and if you are lucky I won't persecute you.

Other negative characteristics:

I like my family and my community to run the same way it always has. I never see the need for change. If it was good enough for my father, then it is good enough for me. I will follow and enforce the status quo.

Inspirational humanitarian

Inspirational humanitarian LightPath

Inspirationals are the world's role models. You respond to the world by wanting to fill a perceived need. As an inspirational, you ask, "What does the world need and how can I provide it?" and "What do you need, and how can I help?"

You have an innate sense of responsibility to yourself, to others and to community, and look at what is needed by both individuals and the group at large. Inspirational SolePaths have the same role as the bones of the body; you provide the structure, the skeleton, the framework for society.

This does not mean that your own needs are lost in your desire to serve, but rather that through your personal learning and experience you feel great empathy with the needs of others and then take action. You inspire us by the way you live your own life and have a great capacity for getting things done to help others.

As an inspirational humanitarian the greatest gift that you share with us is your desire to work for the greater good of all. You work tirelessly for the collective good, righting wrongs. You have a great depth of talent and courage and are a team player when working for a cause that meets your personal beliefs. You have a strong sense of duty and responsibility.

Your core energy as an inspirational humanitarian is: fulfilling my duty and taking action. This core energy represents those positive core values deep within you that create an expansion of your energy; that create inspiring outcomes.

Dr. Debra Ford Msc.D

Being an inspirational humanitarian means finding a cause and then putting a great deal of effort and time into making a difference. You are an active doer who needs to be getting things done, not sitting around talking about what needs to be done.

Who am I?

I respond to the world through my perception of what I think is needed by the group at large. What do you need and how can I help? Inspirational SolePaths have a deep sense of responsibility to the community and are role models for others.

I am called to leave the world a better place! I am an activist. I see the rights of humanity as a whole, as more important than the rights of the individual and work tirelessly for the collective good. I understand that it is my activity that gives me joy, not my success at righting wrongs. I understand that positive change comes slowly but surely.

I confess to being a complicated character. I have an unusual range and depth of talents and am happy to contribute whatever I can to a cause that I believe in. Once I am committed to a cause I feel great empathy with those who are suffering. I have great courage and when I get emotional, I find it difficult to adopt a measured approach (you may see me in handcuffs until I cool down!).

I am very aware of how others are feeling, but usually bottle up my own feelings. As I immerse myself deeper and deeper in a cause, I sometimes neglect my personal life and those I love. I need to learn to say 'no' to avoid burnout and being taken for granted.

My strong sense of duty and responsibility makes me

intolerant of others who I feel are not giving as much as I am to the cause. Perhaps if I loved myself as much as my cause, I would be happier?

What am I doing here?

My Joy comes from taking action to right the wrongs for the collective good. I am combating injustice, I am fighting inequality, I am championing the oppressed, I am defending those groups who can't stand up for themselves.

I have a strong memory for things that are important to the cause. This makes me a great defender of justice as I work tirelessly to create my very clear vision of the way things should be.

Dr. Debra Ford Msc.D

Inspirational humanitarian DarkPath

On the one hand, there is so much about being an inspirational that serves you — you are after all one of the world's role models — and on the other hand there is so much about being a dark inspirational that trips you up.

When you are experiencing your inspirational category from a place of collapsed energy, the overall negative attitude is entitlement and a demand that others obey you. You feel that you are the only one who sees what the world needs and you are certain that your opinions are the only ones that are right. (Even you can see that this is not possible.)

You are intolerant and demand that others look up to you and in the same breath, when you aren't obeyed, complain that you get no support. It must be a throw over from a past life when others were compelled to obey you. Seriously!

Yet, when you are experiencing your inspirational category from a place of expanded energy, you are pretty amazing as you have this deep desire to work towards making a difference in the world.

Who is the humanitarian?

I am very aware of how others are feeling, but usually bottle up my own feelings. As I immerse myself deeper and deeper in a cause, I sometimes neglect my personal life and those I love. I need to learn to say 'no' to avoid burn-out and being taken for granted. My strong sense of duty and responsibility makes me intolerant of others who I feel are not giving as much as I am to the cause. Perhaps if I loved myself as much as my cause, I would be happier? Once I am committed to a cause I feel great empathy with those who are suffering. I have great courage and when I get emotional, I find it difficult to adopt a measured approach (you may see me in handcuffs until I cool down!).

Who is the DarkPath humanitarian?

> The core energy for the dark inspirational humanitarian is neglecting those closest to you. Neglecting your personal life and those you love; feeling that the rights of humanity are more important than the rights of the individual.

I neglect the essential parts of my life, but don't care as I see this is necessary to making the world a better place. For me, charity definitely does not begin at home and I resent my family, friends and co-workers for needing me when I am rescuing the world. I don't really care about those around me, I care about the cause (whatever it is).

I have a warped view of who I need to take care of in this world – if you are close to me it won't be you, but if you are a group of strangers it is probably you. There are no boundaries when I am working on a cause and I get mentally and physically sick. I make myself indispensible to the cause and then resent others who don't recognize how much I am doing, or those who aren't doing as much as me.

Other negative characteristics:

I don't have the ability to take care of relationships and I don't have the ability to take care of myself either.

Dr. Debra Ford Msc.D

Inspirational manager

Inspirational manager LightPath

Inspirationals are the world's role models. You respond to the world by wanting to fill a perceived need. As an inspirational, you ask, "What does the world need and how can I provide it?" and "What do you need, and how can I help?"

You have an innate sense of responsibility to yourself, to others and to community, and look at what is needed by both individuals and the group at large. Inspirational SolePaths have the same role as the bones of the body; you provide the structure, the skeleton, the framework for society.

This does not mean that your own needs are lost in your desire to serve, but rather that through your personal learning and experience you feel great empathy with the needs of others and then take action. You inspire us by the way you live your own life and have a great capacity for getting things done to help others.

As an inspirational manager the greatest gift that you share with us is your extraordinary ability to get things done. You make and implement plans and are a great organizer, supervisor, delegator and participant. You are very competent and proud of your abilities; a little strong willed and always on the go. You really know how to move things forward.

Your core energy as an inspirational manager is: implementation and accomplishment. This core energy represents those positive core values deep within you that create an expansion of your energy; that create inspiring outcomes.

Being an inspirational manager means inspiriting people and managing projects. You understand that people can't be managed but need to be inspired to get things moving forward.

Who am I?

I respond to the world through my perception of what I think is needed by the group at large. What do you need and how can I help? Inspirational SolePaths have a deep sense of responsibility to the community and are role models for others.

Mine is the 'organizer' SolePath. I am at my best when I am organizing, supervising, delegating and participating. I make plans and get them implemented. I am reliable and I easily organize others and develop ways to get things done in a systematic and efficient way.

I know that I am good at what I do; I have a deep confidence and am proud of my abilities (although some may see it as arrogance). I am strong willed and this may seem dictatorial — it's just that I know what the next move is and want it done properly.

I am always on the go and tend to spread myself too thin. I need to get others involved when I get overwhelmed, but this is sometimes difficult for me. I see the perfectionist in me — I demand a lot from myself and from others — but I just have to let others get on with it. I know this about myself and make a concerted effort to positively reinforce what others are doing and try to steer clear of noticing the negative.

Dr. Debra Ford Msc.D

What am I doing here?

My Joy comes from making plans and getting them implemented — any intentions will do. I can clearly see what needs to be done to move things forward. I always know what the next step is and can anticipate what is needed.

I love autonomy and spend a lot of time creating good plans. Having taken the time and done the work to figure out how to proceed, I need people to commit and get on board.

Inspirational manager DarkPath

On the one hand, there is so much about being an inspirational that serves you — you are after all one of the world's role models — and on the other hand there is so much about being a dark inspirational that trips you up.

When you are experiencing your inspirational category from a place of collapsed energy, the overall negative attitude is entitlement and a demand that others obey you. You feel that you are the only one who sees what the world needs and you are certain that your opinions are the only ones that are right. (Even you can see that this is not possible.)

You are intolerant and demand that others look up to you and in the same breath, when you aren't obeyed, complain that you get no support. It must be a throw over from a past life when others were compelled to obey you. Seriously!

Yet, when you are experiencing your inspirational category from a place of expanded energy, you are pretty amazing as you have this deep desire to work towards making a difference in the world.

Who is the manager?

I know that I am good at what I do; I have a deep confidence and am proud of my abilities (although some may see it as arrogance). I am strong willed and this may seem dictatorial — it's just that I know what the next move is and want it done properly.

I am always on the go and tend to spread myself too thin. I need to get others involved when I get overwhelmed, but this is sometimes difficult for me. I see the perfectionist in me — I demand a lot from myself and from others — but I just have to let others get on with it. I love autonomy and spend a lot of time creating good plans. Having taken the time and done the work to figure out how to proceed, I need people to commit and get on board.

Who is the DarkPath manager?

> The core energy for the dark inspirational manager is being a perfectionist. Lacking a belief in others. Being strong willed, dictatorial, intolerant and demanding. Noticing the negative.

I am a perfectionist and whatever you do or say will never be good enough. I am intolerant and demanding and only notice the negative things that you do and say. I won't share what I have and in my absolute arrogance, am quite sure that what I do and say are perfect and right.

Other negative characteristics:

I am strong willed and dictatorial, and don't take what you feel and think into account. I do too much and then resent you for not helping — even though whatever you do will not be good enough.

Inspirational teacher

Inspirational teacher LightPath

Inspirationals are the world's role models. You respond to the world by wanting to fill a perceived need. As an inspirational, you ask, "What does the world need and how can I provide it?" and "What do you need, and how can I help?"

You have an innate sense of responsibility to yourself, to others and to community, and look at what is needed by both individuals and the group at large. Inspirational SolePaths have the same role as the bones of the body; you provide the structure, the skeleton, the framework for society.

This does not mean that your own needs are lost in your desire to serve, but rather that through your personal learning and experience you feel great empathy with the needs of others and then take action. You inspire us by the way you live your own life and have a great capacity for getting things done to help others.

As an inspirational teacher your greatest gift is your ability to communicate so that others can understand. You look for the best in everyone and can find the talent in everyone. You are interested in people and connect in a way that is inspiring, warm, outgoing and enthusiastic.

Your core energy as an inspirational teacher is: talented communicator and inspiring life. This core energy represents those positive core values deep within you that create an expansion of your energy; that create inspiring outcomes.

Being an inspirational teacher means helping others to understand. Teachers are the world's great communicators, however you choose to do this - speaking, writing and by the way you live your life.

Who Am I?

I respond to the world through my perception of what I think is needed by the group at large. What do you need and how can I help? Inspirational SolePaths have a deep sense of responsibility to the community and are role models for others.

I teach by the example of my life. I am dedicated to helping others understand through the example of my life and the ideas that I share. I am a positive person with a 'can-do' attitude. I have a deep understanding that life is what you make of it and I want my life to be inspiring to others.

I am a warm, outgoing, enthusiastic person who willingly gets involved in life. I sometimes feel too much empathy for others and need to remind myself not to take on their difficulties and hardships as my own.

I am not afraid to talk about what I am feeling or to speak my mind and luckily I am a great communicator. I have a natural interest in other people and am very tolerant of them all, no matter how different their lives and beliefs may be from mine.

I do like my life to be organized and I usually schedule things well ahead of time. This allows me to plan and I feel safe within this structure.

What am I doing here?

My Joy comes from helping others understand what I am teaching. I know how to get others to understand and am able to find the talent in everyone. I look for the best in everyone. I usually know what is going on inside a person, I can read others with some accuracy, and I use my interest in them to empower them and to fire up their imagination.

I often speak about my life to inspire others. I didn't always feel this good about myself until I decided that if my life was going to be what I wanted it to be — it was up to me.

Dr. Debra Ford Msc.D

Inspirational teacher DarkPath

On the one hand, there is so much about being an inspirational that serves you – you are after all one of the world's role models – and on the other hand there is so much about being a dark inspirational that trips you up.

When you are experiencing your inspirational category from a place of collapsed energy, the overall negative attitude is entitlement and a demand that others obey you. You feel that you are the only one who sees what the world needs and you are certain that your opinions are the only ones that are right. (Even you can see that this is not possible.)

You are intolerant and demand that others look up to you and in the same breath, when you aren't obeyed, complain that you get no support. It must be a throw over from a past life when others were compelled to obey you. Seriously!

Yet, when you are experiencing your inspirational category from a place of expanded energy, you are pretty amazing as you have this deep desire to work towards making a difference in the world.

Who is the teacher?

I am a warm, outgoing, enthusiastic person who willingly gets involved in life. I sometimes feel too much empathy for others and need to remind myself not to take on their difficulties and hardships as my own.

I often speak about my life to inspire others. I didn't always feel this good about myself until I decided that if my life was going to be what I wanted it to be – it was up to me.

Who is the DarkPath teacher?

> The core energy for the dark inspirational teacher is diminishing and hurting others. Being dismissive, choosing favourites and ostracizing others; being inflexible.

I use my position of authority to diminish and hurt others. Those who look up to me can be scarred by my careless use of words and my dismissive attitude towards them. I am well-known in my own circle and publicly choose favourites leaving others hurt, ostracized and on the outside. I use my ability to read others to find the best way to hurt them. I create cliques to which I belong, but from which I have the power to exclude you.

Other negative characteristics:

I am not spontaneous and have trouble being flexible. I will do anything to take back control in any situation.

Dr. Debra Ford Msc.D

Intellectual SolePaths

Intellectual controller

Intellectual controller LightPath

Intellectuals are the great minds of our world. You respond to the world with logical thought and considerable intelligence. It may be likely that our traditional school system has let you down, so you may not really understand your great mental capacity.

You can trust your ability to think things through and your thought processes are very reliable. There really isn't anything you can't solve when you give yourself enough time and put your mind to it. Your mind points you in the right direction because when you clearly think things through you always know what to do. You get into difficulty when you don't trust this, or allow the opinions of others to get in the way.

As an intellectual controller you are a visionary. You have a strong natural urge to establish structure and give direction in all situations; to create the plan, to set the rules. As a visionary you love to take on responsibility and are a great organizer and coordinator. You are confident and have a great belief in self.

Your core energy as an intellectual controller is: vision to see the future and establishing structure. This core energy represents those positive core values deep within you that create an expansion of your energy; that create thoughtful outcomes.

Being an intellectual controller means that you thrive when you are intellectually stimulated. You are mainly interested in people and information that are relevant to your future projects. You need a quiet focused environment so that you can logically focus on the task or subject at hand (no background music, side conversations or other distractions).

Who am I?

I respond to the world through my mind. I have a considerable intellect that may or may not have been served by the education system. When I trust my brain, I don't make mistakes. There isn't anything that I can't solve when I put my mind to it.

I am a confident person with a great belief in self. I am an example to others; I set the rules; I create the paradigms; I construct the 'box'. People find me very comforting as they know where they stand with me. I love responsibility and find it easy to set priorities. I may sometimes tend towards being authoritarian and have even been called insensitive.

I ensure the efficient and effective use of skills, time and resources. I like things done in a certain way, to save time and wasted effort, and occasionally others may feel that this is restrictive and dictatorial. I sometimes have trouble understanding the emotion that plays such a big part in the lives of others - emotion makes me feel uncomfortable.

I think that I try to control those that I love because I am fearful of life getting out of control and I can also be a jealous person. I struggle with taking responsibility for my situation if it isn't to my liking, and can blame my hardships on others. I usually think that I am right. I have great physical stamina and can usually keep going long after others are exhausted. Controllers don't wait for situations to unfold — and in their need to control everything — are often rude on the phone.

Dr. Debra Ford Msc.D

What am I doing here?

My Joy comes from my strong natural urge to give structure and direction in all situations. I am a great organizer and coordinator. I easily visualize the future and can communicate that vision to others; this in turn allows them to implement agreed goals. I use my intellect to be a great strategist and planner (I don't require too much encouragement to draw up a plan!) and am able to work with both long term and short-term objectives. I only like to work from well thought-out plans and sometimes find it difficult to be flexible if things change. When I am not being true to myself I can step on others to achieve my own goals and under these circumstances feel above the rules that govern others.

Intellectual controller DarkPath

On the one hand, there is so much about being an intellectual that serves you — you are after all one of the world's great minds — and on the other hand there is so much about being a dark intellectual that trips you up.

When you are experiencing your intellectual category from a place of collapsed energy, the overall negative attitude is arrogance and a feeling that everyone else is an idiot. You think that you are the only one who is right and you don't mind making others feel stupid. You use your considerable intellect to tear down and criticize rather than to build up and create. Pity isn't it?

You are good with words and instead of using language to make others feel good, you often take on a condescending tone. It takes you a while to realize that saying the same thing, but in a louder more irritated voice, doesn't usually make what you are saying easier to understand. Seriously!

Yet, when you are experiencing your intellectual category from a place of expanded energy, you contribute to our world with your considerable intellect and your amazing ability to think things through.

Who is the controller?

I ensure the efficient and effective use of skills, time and resources. I like things done in a certain way, to save time and wasted effort, and occasionally others may feel that this is restrictive and dictatorial. I sometimes have trouble understanding the emotion that plays such a big part in the lives of others - emotion makes me feel uncomfortable.

I think that I try to control those that I love because I am

Dr. Debra Ford Msc.D

fearful of life getting out of control and I can also be a jealous person. I struggle with taking responsibility for my situation if it isn't to my liking, and can blame my hardships on others. I usually think that I am right. Controllers don't wait for situations to unfold — and in their need to control everything — are often rude on the phone. I only like to work from well thought-out plans and sometimes find it difficult to be flexible if things change. I may sometimes tend towards being authoritarian and have even been called insensitive. When I am not being true to myself I can step on others to achieve my own goals and under these circumstances feel above the rules that govern others.

Who is the DarkPath controller?

> The core energy for the dark intellectual controller is seeking revenge. Blaming others, acting in a restrictive, dictatorial, authoritarian and insensitive manner.

I am revengeful, I don't forget and I don't forgive. I blame others for the 'ills' in my life and then plot revenge. I don't ever bother to see another's point of view — I simply judge that they are wrong. I use my considerable intellect to create new ways of inflicting harm on others using my words or actions.

Other negative characteristics:

I am formidable and am so certain that I am right, that I am authoritarian and force others to do things and behave in a certain way. I am jealous in romantic relationships, and use my insecurity to control the behaviour of my partner. In most of my relationships I will withhold my love and approval if you don't do what I want in the way that I want it done.

Intellectual expert

Intellectual expert LightPath

Intellectuals are the great minds of our world. You respond to the world with logical thought and considerable intelligence. It may be likely that our traditional school system has let you down, so you may not really understand your great mental capacity.

You can trust your ability to think things through and your thought processes are very reliable. There really isn't anything you can't solve when you give yourself enough time and put your mind to it. Your mind points you in the right direction because when you clearly think things through you always know what to do. You get into difficulty when you don't trust this, or allow the opinions of others to get in the way.

As an intellectual expert you are a specialist. You acquire extensive knowledge that provides clarity and understanding to others. You are highly skilled and insightful in your field and work well alone. You like expert status and recognition, and why not, you have done the work, the study and the research.

Your core energy as an intellectual expert is: desire to acquire knowledge and specialization in one or two fields. This core energy represents those positive core values deep within you that create an expansion of your energy; that create thoughtful outcomes.

Being an intellectual expert means that you thrive on having intimate knowledge of your chosen field of interest. You never skim the surface but rather spend your time researching and specializing in the one or two topics that captivate you. The image is of a pyramid or triangle above your head, distilling the ideas and thoughts that flow from

Dr. Debra Ford Msc.D

your research and learning into a peak of specialization.

Who am I?

I respond to the world through my mind. I have a considerable intellect that may or may not have been served by the education system. When I trust my brain, I don't make mistakes. There isn't anything that I can't solve when I put my mind to it.

I know more about one or two topics than anyone else. I am very intelligent and highly skilled and like to be recognized for what I know. I love to share my knowledge and skills and admit that I enjoy the attention and status that my expert knowledge brings to me. I may seem arrogant and dismissive of those I consider not as learned or as expert as myself. As Muhammad Ali said "I am the Greatest" and I feel the same way about my status in my field.

I am insightful when it comes to my own work and I live in my own world of ideas and theory. When I occasionally question my work, I worry that I haven't done enough to be considered an expert on that subject. On those days I also feel dissatisfied with my achievements.

I may be hard to get to know as I spend a lot of time in my mind. I don't really have much interest in people's feelings and others have difficulty getting to know me. I certainly have trouble with intimacy and with expressing my feelings — they seem so unimportant to me. I often forget to praise others and thank them for the things they do, but this doesn't mean that I don't appreciate them.

What am I doing here?

My Joy comes from acquiring extensive knowledge in a specialized field so that I can provide clarity and understanding to others.

I know that part of my purpose is to theorize, debate, study and research just for the joy of expanding the knowledge base, not only for practical application. I value intelligence, knowledge and efficiency and set high expectations for myself and for others.

Dr. Debra Ford Msc.D

Intellectual expert DarkPath

On the one hand, there is so much about being an intellectual that serves you — you are after all one of the world's great minds — and on the other hand there is so much about being a dark intellectual that trips you up.

When you are experiencing your intellectual category from a place of collapsed energy, the overall negative attitude is arrogance and a feeling that everyone else is an idiot. You think that you are the only one who is right and you don't mind making others feel stupid. You use your considerable intellect to tear down and criticize rather than to build up and create. Pity isn't it?

You are good with words and instead of using language to make others feel good, you often take on a condescending tone. It takes you a while to realize that saying the same thing, but in a louder more irritated voice, doesn't usually make what you are saying easier to understand. Seriously!

Yet, when you are experiencing your intellectual category from a place of expanded energy, you contribute to our world with your considerable intellect and your amazing ability to think things through.

Who is the expert?

I am insightful when it comes to my own work and I live in my own world of ideas and theory. When I occasionally question my work, I worry that I haven't done enough to be considered an expert on that subject. On those days I also feel dissatisfied with my achievements. I set high expectations for myself and for others. I may seem arrogant and dismissive of those I consider not as learned or as expert as myself. As Muhammad Ali said "I am the Greatest" and I feel the same way about my status in my field.

I may be hard to get to know as I spend a lot of time in my mind. I don't really have much interest in people's feelings and others have difficulty getting to know me. I certainly have trouble with intimacy and with expressing my feelings — they seem so unimportant to me. I often forget to praise others and thank them for the things they do.

Who is the DarkPath expert?

> The core energy for the dark intellectual expert is thinking that you can never be nor do enough; being dissatisfied with your achievements. Constantly seeking approval and thinking that you are always lacking.

I feel that I have never done enough; whether it is enough study, enough research or having enough experience; I am always lacking. I am a peculiar mix of arrogance in my intellectual abilities combined with a chronic lack of confidence in my activities. I think I am better than you and look down on those who aren't constantly improving themselves in their personal and business lives. Not only do I believe that I have never done enough, I also believe that you have never done enough — I am disappointed in my achievements and in your achievements.

Other negative characteristics:

Although I never feel worthy of your praise, I constantly seek your demonstrated approval. In this I hold yet another double standard as I never think to praise those around me. I don't and won't understand emotions — they seem so unruly and non-intellectual — I only value what I consider to be intelligence.

Dr. Debra Ford Msc.D

Intellectual lateral thinker

Intellectual lateral thinker LightPath

Intellectuals are the great minds of our world. You respond to the world with logical thought and considerable intelligence. It may be likely that our traditional school system has let you down, so you may not really understand your great mental capacity.

You can trust your ability to think things through and your thought processes are very reliable. There really isn't anything you can't solve when you give yourself enough time and put your mind to it. Your mind points you in the right direction because when you clearly think things through you always know what to do. You get into difficulty when you don't trust this, or allow the opinions of others to get in the way.

As an intellectual lateral thinker you think outside the box. You follow the 180 rule, which is to turn around and look at things from a completely different direction. In this way you are able to encourage new and different ideas. You are an interesting conversationalist who is mentally quick and loves change. You are excited about life and easily acquire new skills.

Your core energy as an intellectual lateral thinker is: innovative thinking and original ideas. This core energy represents those positive core values deep within you that create an expansion of your energy; that create thoughtful outcomes.

Being an intellectual lateral thinker means that you thrive on different ideas. You are captivated by interesting concepts and engaging interaction and conversation with others. The image is of an upside down triangle or funnel above your head, capturing all of the ideas and thoughts that flow into your mind.

Who am I?

I respond to the world through my mind. I have a considerable intellect that may or may not have been served by the education system. When I trust my brain, I don't make mistakes. There isn't anything that I can't solve when I put my mind to it.

With my intellectual lateral thinker SolePath, I think outside the box and create changes in the established and recognized way of doing things.

I am excited and enthusiastic about life and with my intellect find it easy to acquire new skills and knowledge. I am open-minded and flexible and enjoy collaborating with others. I love defining the problem clearly and this leads me to find unique solutions. I break current thinking patterns.

I am a 'why not' person and this makes me an interesting conversationalist. I am mentally quick and love the verbal sparring. I love to debate and have been known to switch to the other side just for the love of it!

Ideas can occupy me completely; I can be busy in my head for hours! I feel great around others who appreciate my intellect and different way of thinking but can feel indifferent and even hostile to those who don't accept new ideas.

Dr. Debra Ford Msc.D

What am I doing here?

My Joy comes from putting innovative ideas into effect. I am aware of possibilities everywhere and am thrilled when I find existing solutions that can be applied in a new and creative way.

Sometimes I reject the 'tried and true' and have new ideas just for the sake of it. I love change! I am not always discriminating about what actually needs to be fixed and can have a 'if it isn't broke, then break it' mentality.

Intellectual lateral thinker DarkPath

On the one hand, there is so much about being an intellectual that serves you — you are after all one of the world's great minds — and on the other hand there is so much about being a dark intellectual that trips you up.

When you are experiencing your intellectual category from a place of collapsed energy, the overall negative attitude is arrogance and a feeling that everyone else is an idiot. You think that you are the only one who is right and you don't mind making others feel stupid. You use your considerable intellect to tear down and criticize rather than to build up and create. Pity isn't it?

You are good with words and instead of using language to make others feel good, you often take on a condescending tone. It takes you a while to realize that saying the same thing, but in a louder more irritated voice, doesn't usually make what you are saying easier to understand. Seriously!

Yet, when you are experiencing your intellectual category from a place of expanded energy, you contribute to our world with your considerable intellect and your amazing ability to think things through.

Who is the lateral thinker?

Ideas can occupy me completely; I can be busy in my head for hours! I feel great around others who appreciate my intellect and different way of thinking but can feel indifferent and even hostile to those who don't accept new ideas.

Sometimes I reject the 'tried and true' and have new ideas just for the sake of it. I love change! I am not always

Dr. Debra Ford Msc.D

discriminating about what actually needs to be fixed and can have a 'if it isn't broke, then break it' mentality.

Who is the DarkPath lateral thinker?

> The core energy for the dark intellectual lateral thinker is being arrogant about your intellect. Having a superior attitude when dealing with others and making them feel uncertain.

I am arrogant and always think that I know better; that I am more intelligent; that I do a better job than anyone else. I am so certain of my superiority that I am often hostile to others for no other reason than that I scorn you because I am smarter than you. I keep my ideas to myself, I withhold my contribution and scorn you because you weren't able to think of my ideas.

Other negative characteristics:

I talk too much and use my words to hurt others and make them feel stupid. You will never know what I believe in, as I switch sides depending on the negative effect it will have on you. I want you to feel uncertain and stupid and this is what makes me feel better about myself.

Intuitive SolePaths

Intuitive builder

Intuitive builder LightPath

Intuitives are the 'gut' reaction SolePaths. You respond to the world through your body. As an intuitive, it is important to identify your body's responses; to know whether a particular sensation means go or stop.

Your body keeps you safe with its immediate reaction to people, situations and experiences. Sometimes it is a feeling in the pit of your stomach, or it may be tingling or goose bumps. When you clearly identify whether the physical sensation you are feeling is 'good' or 'bad' about someone or something, you don't make mistakes. You get into difficulty when you don't trust this, or allow the opinions of others to get in the way.

As an intuitive builder, you are a practical ideas person. You have an extraordinary ability to see the possibilities, to know the end result and how everything fits together. You form things into something better, you organize and connect. You make things happen. You are a tireless ideas person who is also emotional.

Your core energy as an intuitive builder is: seeing possibilities and creating abundance. This core energy represents those positive core values deep within you that create an expansion of your energy; that create positive knowing.

Being an intuitive builder means finding ways to manifest your ideas and networking and connecting people for shared opportunities. It means understanding that you are an emotional yet loving person who is always on the look out for

Dr. Debra Ford Msc.D

the next building block; the next piece of your puzzle. Your greatest fulfillment in seeing your ideas become reality is sharing the abundance of wealth and happiness with others.

Who am I?

I respond to the world through my gut feeling. I can trust my physical (visceral) sensation in the pit of my gut. When I follow my gut feeling, I don't make mistakes. I get into difficulty when I don't trust this and over think, or allow my heart to get in the way. My gut will let me know if I am not trusting my intuition by manifesting 'gut' illness e.g. food allergies, ulcers, constipation, hemorrhoids etc.

I put the pieces together to create something amazing. I see possibilities; I see how everything fits together to create a great end result. I see the quality of raw material and know where it can be used best. I am an ideas person who sees everyone and everything as part of the cosmic whole.

I am a creative ideas person and I trust my own intuition and instincts above all else. I am a participant in life and fun to be around. I am a gentle, warm person who really cares about others. I will do anything to avoid hurting others — both people and animals. Although I am gentle with others, I seem to be very hard on myself and expect excellence at all times.

I am very intuitive — I know things and am not really sure why or how I know them. I feel a bit of a conflict between my intuition (my knowing) and my need for order and structure in my life. I really like my life to be organized and have routine.

I am a deep, complex person who experiences very high and very low emotions. I am sensitive to conflict and problems, both at home and at work. They make me feel very agitated and if I don't have anyone to talk to, this stress can lead to recurring health problems.

What am I doing here?

My Joy comes from gathering the right parts together and creating the whole; I organize and connect. I make things happen by being a tireless worker and I can fit the role of coach or team player as needed. I am able to see problems clearly and easily and I feel fulfilled when I discover the best way to get things done.

A builder should always take a short pause to enjoy their creations, but needs to remember that their joy is in the building, not in the caretaking. New exciting projects await!

Dr. Debra Ford Msc.D

Intuitive builder DarkPath

On the one hand, there is so much about being an intuitive that serves you — you are after all one of those who can recognize and understand your body and gut reaction to the world — and on the other hand there is so much about being a dark intuitive that trips you up.

When you are experiencing your intuitive category from a place of collapsed energy, the overall negative attitude is sabotage. You simply won't trust your own wisdom and your gut and you allow the opinions of others to get in the way. You think that you don't know anything, that everyone else knows better than you and that you always make the wrong decisions. Weird isn't it that you would not listen to your most reliable guide - yourself?

You really do know what is best for you, yet sometimes it seems that you deliberately go out to sabotage your success — wherever it may be, in relationships, at work, anywhere in your life. Stop it!

Yet, when you are experiencing your intuitive category from a place of expanded energy, your guidance is so certain, so reliable and so accurate.

Who is the builder?

I am very intuitive — I know things and am not really sure why or how I know them. I feel a bit of a conflict between my intuition (my knowing) and my need for order and structure in my life. I really like my life to be organized and have routine. I am a deep, complex person who experiences very high and very low emotions.

I am sensitive to conflict and problems, both at home or at

work. They make me feel very agitated and if I don't have anyone to talk to, this stress can lead to recurring health problems

Who is the DarkPath builder?

> The core energy for the dark intuitive builder is dark, uncaring mood swings. Making too much of being a deep complex person and generally feeling discontented with life.

I hold others hostage to my mood swings. When I am unhappy I deliberately create unhappiness for everyone else around me. Intuitively I know the impact that my moods have on those who I live and work with, but I don't care. When I have dark energy around me, I want it to impact you. Why shouldn't you feel as bad as I do?

Other negative characteristics:

I am very hard on myself and discontented with my life and my achievements. I am unable to function when my routine is displaced. I am also unable to function when I sense any conflict around me — at home or at work. I am unable to trust my intuition and constantly question it even when I have absolute proof of trusting my gut-feeling.

Dr. Debra Ford Msc.D

Intuitive creator

Intuitive creator LightPath

Intuitives are the 'gut' reaction SolePaths. You respond to the world through your body. As an intuitive, it is important to identify your body's responses; to know whether a particular sensation means go or stop.

Your body keeps you safe with its immediate reaction to people, situations and experiences. Sometimes it is a feeling in the pit of your stomach, or it may be tingling or goose bumps. When you clearly identify whether the physical sensation you are feeling is 'good' or 'bad' about someone or something, you don't make mistakes. You get into difficulty when you don't trust this, or allow the opinions of others to get in the way.

As an intuitive creator, you are a beautiful ideas person. Your beautiful ideas may manifest as physical things, or may be beautiful conversations, beautiful interactions with others or beautiful experiences. You have an extraordinary ability to manifest original, beautiful creations. Your actions speak louder than your words and you are a sensitive, sometimes serious, naturally reserved and quiet person. You have a strong set of values and pursue your own unique goals.

Your core energy as an intuitive creator is: creating beauty and manifesting ideas. This core energy represents those positive core values deep within you that create an expansion of your energy; that create positive knowing.

Being an intuitive creator means finding ways to make our world more beautiful; your life purpose is to leave our world more beautiful. Your very presence makes the world more beautiful and you have an uncanny ability to explore and share ideas that leave others feeling more beautiful. There is no limit to your creative ideas that include beautiful personal style, beautiful spaces and environments, beautiful experiences. Your greatest fulfillment is creating beauty in the world.

Who am I?

I respond to the world through my gut feeling. I can trust my physical (visceral) sensation in the pit of my gut. When I follow my gut feeling, I don't make mistakes. I get into difficulty when I don't trust this and over think, or allow my heart to get in the way. My gut will let me know if I am not trusting my intuition by manifesting 'gut' illness e.g. food allergies, ulcers, constipation, hemorrhoids etc.

Mine is the 'beautiful' SolePath and I live through all of my five senses. I am an ideas person and I feel that actions speak louder than words. My creations, which are more beautiful than useful, will let you know who I am, what I believe in and what I stand for. I may seem hard to get to know as I am naturally reserved and quiet. I live my life my own way and pursue my own unique goals.

I feel sure that I will find the meaning of life in imaginative, original, beautiful creations. I am sensitive and am very aware of how things look, taste, feel, sound and smell. I avoid making decisions based solely on logic and use my sensitivity, perception and awareness to get me through life.

I take life seriously and my constant search for more beauty may seem like chronic dissatisfaction with 'what is'. I need personal space and time alone to create; I am a bit of a perfectionist so my creations sometimes take a while to manifest. My desire for excellence results in many unfinished projects.

Dr. Debra Ford Msc.D

What am I doing here?

My Joy comes from my unusual gift to manifest imaginative, original, beautiful creations that richly reward my life and the lives of others.

I contribute to a more beautiful, kinder, gentler world and love children and animals (and anyone who needs my love). I genuinely care about others and am sensitive to how they are feeling. I have a desire to be a 'good' person and have a strong set of values, which may seem uncompromising to some.

Intuitive creator DarkPath

On the one hand, there is so much about being an intuitive that serves you — you are after all one of those who can recognize and understand your body and gut reaction to the world — and on the other hand there is so much about being a dark intuitive that trips you up.

When you are experiencing your intuitive category from a place of collapsed energy, the overall negative attitude is sabotage. You simply won't trust your own wisdom and your gut and you allow the opinions of others to get in the way. You think that you don't know anything, that everyone else knows better than you and that you always make the wrong decisions. Weird isn't it that you would not listen to your most reliable guide - yourself?

You really do know what is best for you, yet sometimes it seems that you deliberately go out to sabotage your success — wherever it may be, in relationships, at work, anywhere in your life. Stop it!

Yet, when you are experiencing your intuitive category from a place of expanded energy, your guidance is so certain, so reliable and so accurate.

Who is the creator?

I take life seriously and my constant search for more beauty may seem like chronic dissatisfaction with 'what is'. I need personal space and time alone to create; I am a bit of a perfectionist so my creations sometimes take a while to manifest. My desire for excellence results in many unfinished projects.

I have a desire to be a 'good' person and have a strong set of values, which may seem uncompromising to some. I may seem hard to get to know as I am naturally reserved and quiet. I live my life my own way and pursue my own unique goals

Who is the DarkPath creator?

> The core energy for the dark intuitive creator is dissatisfaction. Being chronically dissatisfied with your life and acting in an uncompromising and unfeeling manner.

I am dissatisfied and disappointed — mostly with you (my friends, my family, my co-workers, my partner). I say that I want love and friendship in my life, but then feel disappointed with you and your silly needs and habits. I am so certain that what I like is right, that your way of living disappoints me. I judge myself to be perfect and I am dissatisfied with you. As far as I am concerned how a person looks is who they are; a person who wears designer clothing is a better person. I judge a book by its cover and if I see you out in the community with a child with un-brushed hair, I know you are a bad parent and even more importantly, I know that I am a better parent than you.

Other negative characteristics:

I don't care about you and don't really want you to care about me; mostly I just want to be left alone. I am very serious and don't seek fun in my life — it seems such a waste of time. I know that I am right. I don't really have any connection to animals.

Intuitive hunter

Intuitive hunter LightPath

Intuitives are the 'gut' reaction SolePaths. You respond to the world through your body. As an intuitive, it is important to identify your body's responses; to know whether a particular sensation means go or stop.

Your body keeps you safe with its immediate reaction to people, situations and experiences. Sometimes it is a feeling in the pit of your stomach, or it may be tingling or goose bumps. When you clearly identify whether the physical sensation you are feeling is 'good' or 'bad' about someone or something, you don't make mistakes. You get into difficulty when you don't trust this, or allow the opinions of others to get in the way.

As an intuitive hunter, you are a truth seeker. You are curious, enquiring and have a thirst for answers and understanding. Once you have found your 'truth' you love to share this knowledge with your community. You are a courageous person who is hard driving and brave, yet also thoughtful and considerate of others. You love the outdoors.

Your core energy as an intuitive hunter is: seeking truth and answers and generosity. This core energy represents those positive core values deep within you that create an expansion of your energy; that create positive knowing.

Being an intuitive hunter means always seeking. Your life flows much like the traditional hunter who was responsible for feeding community. With your courage and bravery you hunt the truth and then return to share this with your community. Because of the energy expended you then need time to sit by the fireside to rejuvenate and it is very important to take time for this rest. Your greatest fulfillment is finding truths to share with others.

Dr. Debra Ford Msc.D

Who am I?

I respond to the world through my gut feeling. I can trust my physical (visceral) sensation in the pit of my gut. When I follow my gut feeling, I don't make mistakes. I get into difficulty when I don't trust this and over think, or allow my heart to get in the way. My gut will let me know if I am not trusting my intuition by manifesting 'gut' illness e.g. food allergies, ulcers, constipation, hemorrhoids etc.

I am a truth seeker. I am curious, inquiring, interested and I have a thirst for understanding. I am generous and happy to share what I know and what I have. I drive myself hard in my constant search for answers. I am brave and am not afraid to pursue what I seek.

I have a great sense of community and enjoy providing. I rely on my intuition to guide me in my life. In most situations I trust my gut reaction above all else and it rarely lets me down. I am thoughtful and considerate of the feelings of others and have an uncanny knack of making others feel at ease. I understand the needs of my community and gather information to share with them.

I love being outdoors; I understand the outdoors and am tuned into nature. Whenever I start to feel stressed or depleted I simply spend time outdoors. I intuitively understand the seasons, the waxing and waning of nature, and love it all.

I live and work in 'spurts' — I need busyness followed by recuperating quiet time and can sometimes find it hard to get going once I am in a down time.

I lose interest in things once I feel I have the answers.

What am I doing here?

My Joy comes from searching; searching for answers; searching for truth and meaning.

I am here to make the world a better place.

Dr. Debra Ford Msc.D

Intuitive hunter DarkPath

On the one hand, there is so much about being an intuitive that serves you — you are after all one of those who can recognize and understand your body and gut reaction to the world — and on the other hand there is so much about being a dark intuitive that trips you up.

When you are experiencing your intuitive category from a place of collapsed energy, the overall negative attitude is sabotage. You simply won't trust your own wisdom and your gut and you allow the opinions of others to get in the way. You think that you don't know anything, that everyone else knows better than you and that you always make the wrong decisions. Weird isn't it that you would not listen to your most reliable guide - yourself?

You really do know what is best for you, yet sometimes it seems that you deliberately go out to sabotage your success — wherever it may be, in relationships, at work, anywhere in your life. Stop it!

Yet, when you are experiencing your intuitive category from a place of expanded energy, your guidance is so certain, so reliable and so accurate.

Who is the hunter?

I love being outdoors; I understand the outdoors and am tuned into nature. Whenever I start to feel stressed or depleted I simply spend time outdoors. I intuitively understand the seasons, the waxing and waning of nature, and love it all.

I live and work in 'spurts' — I need busyness followed by recuperating quiet time and can sometimes find it hard to get going once I am in a down time.

I lose interest in things once I feel I have the answers.

Who is the DarkPath hunter?

> The core energy for the dark intuitive hunter is being unmotivated; living and working in 'spurts' and feeling entitled to be lazy and selfish. Not valuing possessions, your own or those that belong to others.

I am a slob and I just feel entitled to not do anything. I am lazy in my job, I am lazy in taking care of myself, I am lazy when it comes to my family , my home, and my life. I am capable and know that I am – it's just that I don't care about accomplishing anything. Cleanliness, tidiness, basic hygiene take second place to lying around doing nothing – and I don't care how this impacts you.

Other negative characteristics:

I lose interest quickly. I am selfish. I don't value my possessions.

Dr. Debra Ford Msc.D

Intuitive solitude

Intuitive solitude LightPath

Intuitives are the 'gut' reaction SolePaths. You respond to the world through your body. As an intuitive, it is important to identify your body's responses; to know whether a particular sensation means go or stop.

Your body keeps you safe with its immediate reaction to people, situations and experiences. Sometimes it is a feeling in the pit of your stomach, or it may be tingling or goose bumps. When you clearly identify whether the physical sensation you are feeling is 'good' or 'bad' about someone or something, you don't make mistakes. You get into difficulty when you don't trust this, or allow the opinions of others to get in the way.

As an intuitive solitude, you have a great imagination and require quiet to manifest your ideas. You are very comfortable and content when you are alone and able to be yourself. You may be a little unconventional and even a little eccentric, you certainly are independent and introspective and are very self motivated.

Your core energy as an intuitive solitude is: imagination, quietness and contentment. This core energy represents those positive core values deep within you that create an expansion of your energy; that create positive knowing.

Being an intuitive solitude means that much like Beatrix Potter, you love to retreat into quiet so that you can express and manifest your imagination and then return to peaceful and loving interactions with others. Your greatest fulfillment is accessing and manifesting your imagination.

Who am I?

I respond to the world through my gut feeling. I can trust my physical (visceral) sensation in the pit of my gut. When I follow my gut feeling, I don't make mistakes. I get into difficulty when I don't trust this and over think, or allow my heart to get in the way. My gut will let me know if I am not trusting my intuition by manifesting 'gut' illness e.g. food allergies, ulcers, constipation, hemorrhoids etc.

Some may call me a loner. I am most comfortable when I am alone. I am self-sufficient, independent, unconventional and perhaps a little eccentric. I don't care about being popular. I feel good about myself just as I am.

I need time alone to connect with my imagination and to some this may seem anti-social. I don't really understand the emotional needs of others and can suffer withdrawal if I don't find time to be by myself.

I must admit that I find most social interactions to be draining and am really unable to bear small talk. I suppose this makes me introverted, but I am not unfriendly. I have a few carefully chosen intimate friends who I feel confident around and am even quite talkative with.

I sometimes just withdraw from the world. There is nothing wrong with me at these times, I simply need space to rejuvenate and re-connect with my imagination.

What am I doing here?

My Joy comes from accessing my extraordinary imagination, which is a quiet contributor to society. The only way I can access my imagination is to be alone. I am self-motivated and introspective. I use my alone time to explore, with my

Dr. Debra Ford Msc.D

imagination, ideas and thoughts that I am happy to share with others in my own way.

Intuitive solitude DarkPath

On the one hand, there is so much about being an intuitive that serves you — you are after all one of those who can recognize and understand your body and gut reaction to the world — and on the other hand there is so much about being a dark intuitive that trips you up.

When you are experiencing your intuitive category from a place of collapsed energy, the overall negative attitude is sabotage. You simply won't trust your own wisdom and your gut and you allow the opinions of others to get in the way. You think that you don't know anything, that everyone else knows better than you and that you always make the wrong decisions. Weird isn't it that you would not listen to your most reliable guide - yourself?

You really do know what is best for you, yet sometimes it seems that you deliberately go out to sabotage your success — wherever it may be, in relationships, at work, anywhere in your life. Stop it!

Yet, when you are experiencing your intuitive category from a place of expanded energy, your guidance is so certain, so reliable and so accurate.

Who is the solitude?

Some may call me a loner. I am most comfortable when I am alone. I am self-sufficient, independent, unconventional and perhaps a little eccentric. I need time alone to connect with my imagination and to some this may seem anti-social. I don't really understand the emotional needs of others and can suffer withdrawal if I don't find time to be by myself.

I must admit that I find most social interactions to be

Dr. Debra Ford Msc.D

draining and am really unable to bear small talk. I suppose this makes me introverted, but I am not unfriendly.

Who is the DarkPath solitude?

> The core energy for the dark intuitive solitude is being introverted, antisocial and emotionally unavailable. Sometimes holding grudges for years.

I am a sinister loner. If I feel that you are 'against' me, I will plot your demise. When I was on the outside of the group at school, when you ostracized me, I was working out how best to harm you — mentally and physically. I hold grudges and may work on how to hurt you for years before implementing my plan. Because I spend so much time alone and don't have close relationships with others, your perceived wrongs get blown out of proportion in my mind and my plotting and desire to hurt you get magnified.

Other negative characteristics:

I am emotionally unavailable and withhold my affection especially if I feel that you aren't acting in the way that I want you to. I don't know how to share or reciprocate in human interactions and am withdrawn in social situations.

Spiritual SolePaths

Spiritual balance

Spiritual balance LightPath

Spirituals life experience is exploring beliefs and 'what others cannot see' from this physical perspective. To do this, spirituals need to make time to nourish their spiritual connection through meditation and prayer. As a spiritual SolePath you push the boundaries of metaphysical beliefs, much like the intellectual SolePaths push the boundaries of logic and knowledge.

As a spiritual, you can trust your connection. Because you are a spiritual explorer, your beliefs will change over the course of your lifetime. You enjoy the exploration of existing religious and spiritual beliefs as you create your own ideas around faith and the meaning of life.

As a spiritual balance, your gift to the world is showing us how to go with the flow. Your ability to create balance in your own life inspires us to find balance too. You are dependable, stable and love harmony. You have a genuine love of people and are warm, friendly, kind-hearted and generous.

Your core energy as a spiritual balance is: going with the flow and living with grace. This core energy represents those positive core values deep within you that create an expansion of your energy; that create positive, connected feelings.

Being a spiritual balance means flowing downstream and not resisting the flow of life. You love harmony and positive environments and know how to create those for yourself and for others. You understand that life can be simple when distractions are eliminated and all of us are flowing

Dr. Debra Ford Msc.D

downstream.

Who am I?

I respond to the world through my connection to that 'bigger' part of me. When I am connected to what I believe in, I can trust that guidance. I get into difficulty when I don't trust my connection and over think, or allow my heart to get in the way. I need to make time to nourish my connection.

I am happiest when I am going with the flow. I am dependable, stable and have great poise. When others look at me, they say "She/he has real class" and I am very proud of that. My greatest gift is that I am able to 'go with the flow' and this makes me confident, content and satisfied with life.

For my peace of mind, I need things to run smoothly both at home and at work. I sometimes go overboard in trying to avoid conflict and forget that you can't always please both sides. I sometimes have difficulty coping when there is too much change in my life. I am a deliberate thinker and change can make me feel stressed and it usually has a physical impact on my body. When I feel stressed I withdraw into myself and need to remember to reach out to others who can help.

I have excellent people skills and a genuine love of other people. I am described as warm, friendly, kind-hearted and generous. I love beautiful things around me and really appreciate beauty in nature.

I mostly live in the here and now and as I go with the flow, I enjoy everything that I do — my relationships, my home, my job and my community. I feel that it is important to be a 'model citizen'. I don't usually rock the boat and like to honour traditions and the law. I have my own clear set of standards and beliefs, but accept the differences of others. I don't make a fuss or invent problems.

What am I doing here?

My Joy comes from going with the flow. As I find balance and equilibrium in my own life, this has a positive influence on others around me. I love harmony and can usually see both sides of an issue as I easily understand another's perspective and feelings. This helps me to easily and competently settle misunderstandings and restore calm. I like to bring others together and gather them around me and am especially fond of children and animals. I am also a great team player and am non-judgmental and relaxed, but do expect others to live honourable lives.

Dr. Debra Ford Msc.D

Spiritual balance DarkPath

On the one hand, there is so much about being a spiritual that serves you – you are, after all, one of the people most connected to non-physical energy – and on the other hand there is so much about being a dark spiritual that trips you up.

When you are experiencing your spiritual category from a place of collapsed energy, the overall negative attitude is superiority. You are dogmatic about your own beliefs and completely unaccepting about the beliefs of others. Not only do you feel that your beliefs are the only ones that are right, you are unwilling to look at another's perspective. It doesn't matter whether your beliefs are fundamental religion or the most liberal spirituality – your way is the right way.

You are a judgmental observer, standing on the sidelines of life, not participating yet judging others as wrong. It would be great fun for you to get in the game. Really!

Yet, when you are experiencing your spiritual category from a place of expanded energy, you contribute to our world with your spiritual exploring, you make it okay for us to believe in something 'bigger than ourselves', you push the boundaries of belief.

Who is the balance?

I am a great team player and am non-judgmental and relaxed, but do expect others to live honourable lives. For my peace of mind, I need things to run smoothly both at home and at work. I sometimes go overboard in trying to avoid conflict and forget that you can't always please both sides. I sometimes have difficulty coping when there is too much change in my life.

I am a deliberate thinker and change can make me feel stressed and it usually has a impact on my body. When I feel stressed I withdraw into myself and need to remember to reach out to others who can help.

Who is the DarkPath balance?

> The core energy for the dark spiritual balance is being unable to make a decision. You don't commit to anything or anyone and have no remorse for letting others down. Trying to get a decision out of a dark balance is like trying to grab a handful of water.

I will let you down as I am unable to make a decision – ever. I look at all sides of an issue, unendingly and never stand for anything; am never committed to anything. I cannot stand by your side because I cannot make a decision, and am afraid of offending anyone. I change my mind with whatever new piece of information comes in and you will never know where you stand with me.

You can never rely on me for anything. Knowing me is like trying to grab hold of a handful of water and I feel no remorse for letting you down, whatever the consequences for you. It's your fault you asked me to hold the ladder, even though I am the one that got distracted and walked away.

Other negative characteristics:

I resist change as I can't cope with it. I use physical illness to manipulate you – usually a headache - and withdraw into my own world with no regard for the impact it has on you. I tend towards obsessive-compulsive behaviour.

Dr. Debra Ford Msc.D

Spiritual mystic

Spiritual mystic LightPath

Spirituals life experience is exploring beliefs and 'what others cannot see' from this physical perspective. To do this, spirituals need to make time to nourish their spiritual connection through meditation and prayer. As a spiritual SolePath you push the boundaries of metaphysical beliefs, much like the intellectual SolePaths push the boundaries of logic and knowledge.

As a spiritual, you can trust your connection. Because you are a spiritual explorer, your beliefs will change over the course of your lifetime. You enjoy the exploration of existing religious and spiritual beliefs as you create your own ideas around faith and the meaning of life.

As a spiritual mystic, your gift to the world is your spiritual exploration, actively elevating humanities spiritual energy. You are connected to source energy and to your higher self. You have a talent for the written and spoken word and can communicate your spiritual experiences. You have a deep need for solitude and quiet private time.

Your core energy as a spiritual mystic is: spirituality and connection. This core energy represents those positive core values deep within you that create an expansion of your energy; that create positive, connected feelings.

Being a spiritual mystic means exploring the religious and spiritual beliefs of others and then deciding what you will believe in. Being a spiritual mystic means making spiritual exploration acceptable to others. Being a spiritual mystic means sharing your findings, new understandings and mystical experiences with others. Being a spiritual mystic means understanding that your beliefs will change over the course of your lifetime.

Who am I?

I respond to the world through my connection to that 'bigger' part of me. When I am connected to what I believe in, I can trust that guidance. I get into difficulty when I don't trust my connection and over think, or allow my heart to get in the way. I need to make time to nourish my connection.

Mine is the spiritual SolePath. I am a spiritual being; I know that I am more than my physical body; I know that I made a deliberate decision to have a physical experience on Earth.

I know what I believe in. I know the answers to the questions "Who am I?" and "What am I doing here?" At my best I am willing to talk of my beliefs to others and allow them to create their own set of beliefs. At my worst I am judgmental and unwilling to accept different beliefs. I may be allowing or I may be dogmatic; I may be humble or I may be arrogant; I may be unassuming or I may act superior.

I have a real need for solitude, for quiet private time. This is my time to re-connect with source energy, to recharge my batteries, to strengthen myself for the task of raising the spiritual energy of the world. I sometimes have real difficulty living in the 'here and now' of the physical world.

I have strong personal charisma, which attracts others to me, but I can't tolerate superficial personal interactions (I am terrible at small talk). I am hard to get to know as I am a very private person and tend not to share my innermost thoughts or emotions, except on spiritual matters, unless with a select few trusted friends. I am highly intuitive and understand non-verbal communications.

Dr. Debra Ford Msc.D

What am I doing here?

My joy is to promote people's belief in something "bigger than themselves" and show them how to understand their connection with God and Source Energy. I understand my own connection to God and Source Energy and use this understanding to inform, inspire, stimulate and elevate humanity.

My talent for the spoken and written word allows me to communicate in a personalized way so that others understand my message.

Spiritual mystic DarkPath

On the one hand, there is so much about being a spiritual that serves you — you are, after all, one of the people most connected to non-physical energy — and on the other hand there is so much about being a dark spiritual that trips you up.

When you are experiencing your spiritual category from a place of collapsed energy, the overall negative attitude is superiority. You are dogmatic about your own beliefs and completely unaccepting about the beliefs of others. Not only do you feel that your beliefs are the only ones that are right, you are unwilling to look at another's perspective. It doesn't matter whether your beliefs are fundamental religion or the most liberal spirituality — your way is the right way.

You are a judgmental observer, standing on the sidelines of life, not participating yet judging others as wrong. It would be great fun for you to get in the game. Really!

Yet, when you are experiencing your spiritual category from a place of expanded energy, you contribute to our world with your spiritual exploring, you make it okay for us to believe in something 'bigger than ourselves', you push the boundaries of belief.

Who is the mystic?

I know what I believe in. I know the answers to the questions "Who am I?" and "What am I doing here?" At my best I am willing to talk of my beliefs to others and allow them to create their own set of beliefs; at my worst I am judgmental and unwilling to accept different beliefs. I may be allowing or I may be dogmatic; I may be humble or I may be arrogant; I may be unassuming or I may act superior. I sometimes have real difficulty living in the 'here and now' of the physical world.

I have strong personal charisma, which attracts others to me, but I can't tolerate superficial personal interactions (I am terrible at small talk). I am hard to get to know as I am a very private person and tend not to share my innermost thoughts or emotions unless with a select few trusted friends.

Who is the DarkPath mystic?

> The core energy for the dark spiritual mystic is being judgmental, superior and arrogant. You are intolerant and unwilling to accept the beliefs of others and are dogmatic about your own beliefs.

I am judgmental and unwilling to accept the beliefs of others. I hold others to a different standard and expect them to accept my beliefs. I am dogmatic about beliefs and unable to consider another point of view. I am arrogant about my own beliefs and am certain that I am a superior human being to you. I have a "don't do as I do, do as I say" mentality. I easily neglect others in my life, because 'god' said so. Taking care of those who believe as I do, my congregation or group is much more important than taking care of my family. I lose perspective on life and forget that it is a physical life and not all about my spiritual dogma.

Other negative characteristics:

I have no real friends as I am intolerant and usually watch others to see if they are doing something wrong, acting outside of my rigid belief system. I can't tolerate superficial interactions and don't like to talk about anything else except my beliefs and how to punish those who don't follow them. I don't allow others in and am hard to get to know.

Spiritual warrior

Spiritual warrior LightPath

Spirituals life experience is exploring beliefs and 'what others cannot see' from this physical perspective. To do this, spirituals need to make time to nourish their spiritual connection through meditation and prayer. As a spiritual SolePath you push the boundaries of metaphysical beliefs, much like the intellectual SolePaths push the boundaries of logic and knowledge.

As a spiritual, you can trust your connection. Because you are a spiritual explorer, your beliefs will change over the course of your lifetime. You enjoy the exploration of existing religious and spiritual beliefs as you create your own ideas around faith and the meaning of life.

As a spiritual warrior, your gift to the world is dedication to your spiritual cause. You hold deep convictions and will stand up for what you believe in. You are deeply connected and the only truly psychic SolePath. You have great integrity and can be counted on. You are capable and organized and have a tremendous amount of energy when working for your cause and what you believe in.

Your core energy as a spiritual warrior is: integrity and dedication and psychic ability. This core energy represents those positive core values deep within you that create an expansion of your energy; that create positive, connected feelings.

Being a spiritual warrior means that you are the spiritual SolePath with attitude; you are the mystic with sharp elbows. Your cause will change over the course of your lifetime and when you choose where to put your energy and effort, you are tireless.

Dr. Debra Ford Msc.D

Who am I?

I respond to the world through my connection to that 'bigger' part of me. When I am connected to what I believe in, I can trust that guidance. I get into difficulty when I don't trust my connection and over think, or allow my heart to get in the way. I need to make time to nourish my connection.

I need a cause! I am at my best when I am standing up for a cause that I believe in. I hold deep convictions about what I consider to be the important things in life. I inspire others; I am dedicated to my cause; I am committed to my beliefs and the life that I lead reflects this. I walk the talk!

I am a very private person who is connected to higher self, is intuitive and psychic.

I have a strong sense of duty, am serious minded and am always motivated to follow through. If I make a commitment to a worthwhile cause I can always be counted on. I put a tremendous amount of energy and effort into doing any task that I see as important and moves my cause forward; I just can't put any energy into anything I don't fully believe in. I can be seen as uncompromising and will usually have many causes over the course of my lifetime.

I am a capable, organized person who has been successful at most of the things I have undertaken in my life. I work hard, I have deep drive and I don't allow obstacles to get in my way. I prefer to think alone and am always accountable for my actions. I may sometimes be impatient with others if they get in the way. I might be described as a mystic with attitude and can sometimes be perceived as uncompromising.

What am I doing here?

My joy comes from dedicating myself to a cause that I believe in and the earlier in my life that I discover my cause, the more joyful my life becomes.

I am always on the front lines for my cause and others are inspired by me.

I am able to take insightful action and find unique solutions for my cause. I like to have a plan but I don't allow it to stifle my creativity or stop me getting things done. I am a rebel with a cause.

Dr. Debra Ford Msc.D

<u>Spiritual warrior DarkPath</u>

On the one hand, there is so much about being a spiritual that serves you — you are, after all, one of the people most connected to non-physical energy — and on the other hand there is so much about being a dark spiritual that trips you up.

When you are experiencing your spiritual category from a place of collapsed energy, the overall negative attitude is superiority. You are dogmatic about your own beliefs and completely unaccepting about the beliefs of others. Not only do you feel that your beliefs are the only ones that are right, you are unwilling to look at another's perspective. It doesn't matter whether your beliefs are fundamental religion or the most liberal spirituality — your way is the right way.

You are a judgmental observer, standing on the sidelines of life, not participating yet judging others as wrong. It would be great fun for you to get in the game. Really!

Yet, when you are experiencing your spiritual category from a place of expanded energy, you contribute to our world with your spiritual exploring, you make it okay for us to believe in something 'bigger than ourselves', you push the boundaries of belief.

Who is the warrior?

I have a strong sense of duty, am serious minded and am always motivated to follow through. I put a tremendous amount of energy and effort into doing any task that I see as important and moves my cause forward; I just can't put any energy into anything I don't fully believe in. I can be seen as uncompromising and will usually have many causes over the course of my lifetime.

I may sometimes be impatient with others if they get in the way. I might be described as a mystic with attitude.

Who is the DarkPath warrior?

> The core energy for the dark spiritual warrior is being uncompromising. You are impatient and unfeeling and can walk over others; you won't allow anything to get in your way.

I am a cold heartless person who only cares about my 'cause'. I determine what my cause is and you can't influence me in this. I won't let anything get in my way, not my family, nor my friends. I will walk all over you regardless of the consequences.

I choose my cause because of what it can do for me and my personal standing. I deem my cause to be inviolate and despise you for not having the same dedication and vision as me.

Other negative characteristics:

I don't allow others into my life, unless they can help me move my cause forward. I am uncompromising, impatient, unfeeling and don't usually like animals and children unless they are useful to my personal acclaim.

Dr. Debra Ford Msc.D

Dr. Debra Ford Msc.D

ABOUT THE AUTHOR

Dr. Debra is a spiritual philosophy teacher with a doctorate in metaphysical science. She is an ordained minister and a member of the american metaphysical doctors association and the canadian institute of metaphysical ministers.

Dr. Debra's SolePath is inspirational teacher and spiritual mystic. It is this SolePath that allows her to connect, create and communicate the SolePath original body of work. Her core values and core energy are spirituality and connection, inspiration and communication.

Dr. Debra Ford is the co-founder of the SolePath institute, along with her husband John. The SolePath institute joyfully encourages everyone to know and understand their SolePath and live a beautiful life filled with purpose and meaning.

Our purpose at the SolePath institute is to ask how may we serve you, how can we help?

How may we encourage you on your path to a beautiful life filled with purpose? How may we assist you as you manifest your body of work?

We are certain that there is a great truth within you, a teaching that will contribute to the change that we are all intending for our world.

The SolePath institute is dedicated to the development and understanding of SolePath, including:

- Assisting with the manifestation of your great truth
- SolePath research, development and training
- SolePath energy analysis
- SolePath library of records

What is your work? How may we help? We are actively looking for collaborators who want to layer SolePath onto their work.

Dr. Debra Ford Msc.D

CONTACT

Website: www.SolePath.org

Email: info@SolePath.org

Mailing address: the SolePath institute, 716 brookpark
drive sw, calgary, alberta, canada, t2w 2x4

Helpline: 403.998.0191

27060621R00179

Made in the USA
Charleston, SC
01 March 2014